How to Not Write Bad

Also by Ben Yagoda

Memoir: A History

When You Catch an Adjective, Kill It:
The Parts of Speech, for Better and/or Worse

The Sound on the Page: Style and Voice in Writing

About Town: The New Yorker *and the World It Made*

Will Rogers: A Biography

The Art of Fact: A Historical Anthology of
Literary Journalism (coeditor)

All in a Lifetime: An Autobiography (with Ruth Westheimer)

How to Not Write Bad

The Most Common
Writing Problems and
the Best Ways to
Avoid Them

BEN YAGODA

RIVERHEAD BOOKS
New York

RIVERHEAD BOOKS
Published by the Penguin Group
Penguin Group (USA) Inc.
375 Hudson Street, New York, New York 10014, USA
Penguin Group (Canada), 90 Eglinton Avenue East, Suite 700, Toronto, Ontario M4P 2Y3, Canada
(a division of Pearson Penguin Canada Inc.) • Penguin Books Ltd., 80 Strand, London WC2R 0RL,
England • Penguin Ireland, 25 St. Stephen's Green, Dublin 2, Ireland (a division of Penguin
Books Ltd.) • Penguin Group (Australia), 707 Collins Street, Melbourne, Victoria 3008, Australia
(a division of Pearson Australia Group Pty. Ltd.) • Penguin Books India Pvt. Ltd., 11 Community
Centre, Panchsheel Park, New Delhi—110 017, India • Penguin Group (NZ), 67 Apollo Drive,
Rosedale, Auckland 0632, New Zealand (a division of Pearson New Zealand Ltd.) • Penguin Books
(South Africa), Rosebank Office Park, 181 Jan Smuts Avenue, Parktown North 2193, South Africa •
Penguin China, B7 Jiaming Center, 27 East Third Ring Road North,
Chaoyang District, Beijing 100020, China

Penguin Books Ltd., Registered Offices: 80 Strand, London WC2R 0RL, England

The publisher does not have any control over and does not assume any responsibility for
author or third-party websites or their content.

First Riverhead trade paperback edition: February 2013

ISBN: 978-1-59448-848-1

Library of Congress Cataloging-in-Publication Data

Yagoda, Ben.
How to Not Write Bad / Ben Yagoda.—First Riverhead edition.
pages cm
ISBN 978-1-59448-848-1
1. English language—Rhetoric—Handbooks, manuals, etc. 2. Report writing—Handbooks,
manuals, etc. 3. English language—Grammar—Handbooks, manuals, etc. I. Title.
PE1408.Y34 2013
808'.042—dc23 2012043126

PRINTED IN THE UNITED STATES OF AMERICA

10 9 8 7 6

To David Friedman
with thanks for being in my corner all these years

CONTENTS

CONTENTS

How to Not
Write Bad

INTRODUCTION

Why a book on how to not write bad (or badly, if you insist)?

I'm glad you asked. Simply put, this is a crucial and seriously underrepresented county in the Alaska-size state of books about writing. From the all-time champ, Strunk and White's *The Elements of Style*, through more touchy-feely works like Anne Lamott's *Bird by Bird*, texts on this subject virtually all have the same goal. Sometimes it's implicit, and sometimes it's right there in the title, as in William Zinsser's classic guide, *On Writing Well*.

That emphasis is fine, but it has its limitations. In a way, it reminds me of the "vanity sizing" favored by the apparel industry—the custom of labeling thirty-four-inch-waist pants as thirty-two so as to make customers feel good about themselves (and buy that company's pant, needless to say). I have spent the last twenty years teaching advanced journalism and writing classes in a selective university, and the majority of my (bright) students put me in mind of what Jack Nicholson famously shouted to Tom Cruise in *A Few Good Men*. The Cruise character couldn't *handle* the truth, Nicholson said. Well, most students, I've found, can't *handle* writing "well." At this point in their writing lives, that goal is simply too ambitious.

It's not just my students, either. My colleagues at various institutions say they encounter the same problems I do. And I've run into these issues when I've taught workshops all over the country and, of course, in that new and universal forum for written expression of every conceivable kind, the Internet.

You can certainly understand why people would want to aim high, especially in the United States, where self-esteem is fed to toddlers along with their Cheerios, and all the children are apparently above average. But you have to crawl before you walk, and walk before you run. And you have to be able to put together a clear and at least borderline graceful sentence, and to link that sentence with another one, before you can expect to make like David Foster Wallace.

In the 1950s, the British psychoanalyst Donald Winnicott coined the term *good-enough mother* (now more commonly and equitably expressed as *good-enough parent*). It's proved to be an enduring and very useful concept, referring to mothers and fathers who don't have superpowers, who can't solve every problem and address every need of their children, who make mistakes, but who provide a level of attention, concern, and care that may seem merely adequate but that turns out to do the job quite well. What I'm talking about here is good-enough writing. As with parenting, it isn't necessarily easy to achieve, but it's definitely achiev*able*. And it's a decidedly worthwhile goal.

* * *

Words are the building blocks of sentences, and sentences are the building blocks of any piece of writing; consequently, I focus on these basics. As far as I'm concerned, not-writing-badly consists of the ability, first, to craft sentences that are correct in terms of spelling, diction (that is, word choice), punctuation, and grammar, and that display clarity, precision, and grace. Once that's mastered, there are a few more areas that have to be addressed in crafting a whole paragraph: cadence, consistency of tone, word repetition, transitions between sentences, paragraph length. And that's all there is to it! (I know, I know, that's plenty.)

I've mentioned my students but this book isn't just for classroom use. It's for everyone who wants to improve his or her prose. Let me be more precise. The best way to measure or think about the badness of a sentence, or an entire piece of writing, is to imagine the effect it has on someone who reads it. This could be a teacher or professor; an editor who's deciding whether to publish it in a magazine; a hypothetical person out in cyberspace who has just come upon a new blog post; or a coworker confronted with an interoffice memo. In all cases, bad writing will induce boredom, annoyance, incomprehension, and/or daydreaming. The less bad it is, the more that real or imaginary soul will experience the text as clear, readable, persuasive, and, in the best case, pleasing. And the more that reader will keep on reading.

The book is also for high school and college teachers. Not only are they weary of writing "awkward," "comma splice," "faulty parallelism," "dangling modifier," and such over and over again on student work, they have good reason to fear that stating and restating these epithets is as hurtful as name-calling and just about as effective in changing someone's ways. Directing students to the appropriate entry in the book, by contrast, may actually help them learn what they're doing wrong and how to address the issue.

In the last couple of paragraphs, I talked about things like *clarity*, *precision*, and *grace*, about a text being *clear*, *readable*, *persuasive*, and *pleasing*. You will rarely hear such words from me again, at least in this book. It operates on the counterintuitive premise that the best road to those goals is by way of avoiding their opposites. Telling someone how to write well is like gripping a handful of sand; indeed, the sheer difficulty of the task may be why there are so many books on the subject. An analogy is with a nation's or state's laws. They don't say, *Be considerate to others* or *Give money to charity* or even a Jerry Lewis statute like *Be a nice lady!* Instead, they are along the lines of *Do not lie on your income tax return* or *Do not shoot or stab individuals*. The thinking is that if bad behavior is proscribed, good behavior will emerge. (Western religions are a little more willing to tell you what *to* do, but not that much so. The only positive two of the Ten Commandments are number four, "Remember the Sabbath day to keep it holy," and five, "Honor your father and your mother.")

Consequently, this book is mainly about the things that writing badly entails. For example, I don't tell you, *Be sure to choose the right word*. It's not that I disagree with that—how could I? It's rightfully a staple of how-to-write-well books, often accompanied by a spot-on Mark Twain quote: "The difference between the almost right word & the right word is really a large matter—it's the difference between the lightning bug and the lightning." Good stuff and good advice, but how the heck are you supposed to carry it out? Here, in a nutshell, is my "accentuate the negative" approach to word choice:

1. Don't use a long word when there's a shorter one that means the same thing.

2. Avoid word repetition. Do not avoid it by means of "elegant variation"—the use of a synonym for the express purpose of avoiding word repetition. (If the original sentence is, "The boy I'm babysitting tomorrow is usually a well-behaved boy," the elegant varyer would change the last word to "lad.") Rather, use pronouns and/or recast the whole sentence—in the example above, "The boy I'm babysitting tomorrow is usually well behaved."

3. If you are considering a word about whose spelling or meaning you have even a scintilla of doubt, look it up.

And you're on your way.

You are holding a slim volume in your hands. (If you're holding an electronic device in your hands, you'll have to trust me on this one.) That's because the body of common current writing problems isn't very big. On the basis of some back-of-the-envelope ciphering, I conclude that I've read and graded something like 10,000 pieces of written work over the last two decades—articles, reviews, memos, research papers, essays, memoirs, and more, from a fairly diverse (in skill, intelligence, training, interests, and background) group of students. Maybe 95 percent of the corrections and comments I make on their work have to do with about fifty errors and problems. Those are the entries in *How to Not Write Bad*. If you master them, you might not be David Foster Wallace, but you'll be ahead of almost all your fellow writers.

The nature of the fabulous fifty may be a little surprising; a lot of them don't get much press. Even when they do try to address common writing errors, most writing guides and handbooks are off the mark, it seems to me. Often, they display a weird time lag. I remember being puzzled in junior high school to read in my grammar book that it's incorrect to write of someone "setting" in a chair, rather than "sitting." No one I knew in New Rochelle, New York, ever talked of "setting" in a chair. Only later, after becoming familiar with *The Beverly Hillbillies* and Ma and Pa Kettle films, did I realize that the reference was to a widespread rural locution of the forties and fifties.

Fast-forward to the second decade of the twenty-first century. The most (deservedly) popular writing guide is *The Elements of Style*, based on a pamphlet Will Strunk distributed to his Cornell students circa 1918. E. B. White updated it in 1959, and subsequent editions have made minimal changes. Rule 6 of Part I ("Elementary Rules of Usage") is "Do not break sentences in two," and the example given is, "I met them on a Cunard liner many years ago. Coming home from Liverpool to New York." The trouble is not merely that almost everyone born after 1950 will be mystified by the phrase *Cunard liner*; it is also that twenty-first-century American citizens almost never are guilty of this particular kind of sentence fragment. Don't ask me why. They just aren't. Another Strunk and White example of what not to do is this sentence: "Your dedicated whittler requires: a knife, a piece of wood, and a back porch." Again, leave aside the sketchy cultural reference to dedicated whittlers. The problem here is that standards have changed such that a colon after anything but a complete sentence—the problem, to S. & W.—is now kosher. You might disagree with me on this, but you have to grant that to the extent it is a problem, it's one that comes up extremely rarely. (The *your* + *noun* formulation— "Your dedicated whistler"—has pretty much gone by the boards as well.)

Then there are the more comprehensive writing books, such as *The Bedford Handbook*, which I have right in front of me and which qualifies for the final word in its title only if you have a really big hand. That is, it's long—818 pages, plus index. It aims, as the second sentence in it says, to "answer most of the questions you are likely to ask as you plan, draft, and revise a piece of writing." I'll say. Pretty much everything is in here: common mistakes, uncommon mistakes, and lots of things that all people who grew up speaking English (and lots of nonnative speakers as well) know without giving them a second thought. Plus, it goes for $56.59 on amazon.com.

How to Not Write Bad has three parts. Part I gives and expands on a one-word answer to the challenge posed by the title, and goes on to talk more generally about what it means to be a not-bad writer. Parts II and III explain the most common writing problems and give examples I've taken from actual student assignments. Part III (to jump ahead for a second) deals with writing choices that aren't strictly speaking wrong but are, well, ill-advised: awkwardness, wordiness, unfortunate word choice, bad rhythm, clichés, dullness, and the other most frequently committed crimes against good prose.

The mistakes in Part II are, literally, *mistakes*: of punctuation, spelling, wording, and grammar. There's a lot of talk afoot about "grammatical errors," so you might be surprised to find that grammar is the least of the problem, as I see it. Misspelled or just-plain-wrong words and train-wreck punctuation have gotten more prevalent over the years, for reasons I'll get into later. And spelling and punctuation (more so than grammar) follow hard-and-fast rules, so there really is a clear sense of right and wrong.

As for grammar or syntax, linguists are fond of saying that a native speaker is incapable of making a grammatical mistake. Linguists are also fond of exaggerating, but they have a point, up to a point. No one born and raised in this country would say or write, *He gave I the book,* and to the extent that a book like *The Bedford Handbook* explains why the third word in that sentence should be *me,* it is wasting paper and ink and its readers' time. In my experience, students are generally aware of and comfortable with grammatical standards. They tend to go off course in a relatively small number of areas (all of which are attended to in Part II). That would include: use of subjunctive (*If I was/were king*), pronoun choice (*He gave the books to John and I; Who/whom did you speak to?*), dangling modifiers (*Before coming to class today, my car broke down*), subject-verb agreement (*A group of seniors were/was chosen to receive awards*), and parallelism (*We ate sandwiches, coleslaw, and watched the concert*).*

Beyond these and a couple of others, most recurring grammar issues are fine points. That is, they are easily corrected or looked up and don't have much bearing on writing or not writing badly.

---

* Full marks, by the way, if you noticed that in this sentence I broke Strunk and White's colon rule.

What's more, accepted practice will probably change fairly soon so as to condone what the student has done. (Now, if you are *not* a native speaker or if you are don't have some of the important rudiments of grammar, spelling, and so forth, you need something more basic than this book. *The Bedford Handbook* or a similar reference work would be a good place to start.)

On that idea of "accepted practice" changing, I recognize—as how could anyone not?—that standards evolve over time. There was a time when it was verboten to end a sentence with a preposition, start one with a conjunction, write *an e-mail* instead of *an e-mail message*, use *hopefully* to mean *I hope that,* and so on. Now all those things are okay. Going back even further, it used to be that the first-person future tense of *to go* was thought to be *I shall go.* If you said that today, you would get some seriously strange looks. *Awful* used to refer to the quality of filling one with, you guessed it, awe; now it means really bad.

But it takes time to change a standard. The mere fact that a substantial number of people do something doesn't make it right. Take the title of this book. It splits an infinitive, which used to be wrong but isn't anymore. It also says (for comic effect) *Bad* instead of *Badly.* That used to be wrong and still is. Same with something that an unaccountably large number of my students have taken to doing over the past few years; using a semicolon when they should use a colon, the way I just did. Still wrong. So is another strange and new predilection, spelling the past tense of the verb *to lead* as *lead.* I would guess it's so popular because (A) spell-check says it's okay and (B) people are misled by the spelling of two words that rhyme with *led*: the metal *lead* and the past-tense *read.* In any case, that semicolon use and that spelling may one day attain the acceptance of a split infinitive, but they haven't yet. (Less than two hours after I wrote those words, I read a *New York Times* article with the words "what most troubled her was how he had *mislead* the public." The change may come sooner than I think!)

Generally speaking, it's fairly easy to figure out current standards. But a few things are trickier because they are right on the cusp of change. I make judgment calls on these. Probably the best current example is the use of *they* or *their* as a singular pronoun—in sentences like *Anyone who wants to go to the concert should bring their money tomorrow* or *I like Taco Bell because they serve enchiladas that are oozing with cheese.* The usage is almost completely prevalent in spoken English, in British written English (interestingly enough), in online publications, and, it almost goes without saying, in blogs and e-mails. I predict it will be accepted in American publishing within ten years. But it isn't yet, and so for my purposes it counts as bad writing.

I mentioned that I mainly take my corpus of writing problems from student papers. Almost all the same things can be seen in the writing world at large. Not so much in books and newspaper and magazine articles, but rather in e-mails, blog posts, comments, and other online documents. These texts are not selected or processed by an editor (and are for the most part not the work of professionals) and thus display in a clear light the way we write now.

Taken collectively, this collection of problems and errors is kind of strange. I think of it as a giant blob of writing woe, slowly shifting as the years pass. To be sure, there have been some constants over the past two decades. When I started teaching, I wasn't even familiar with the term *comma splice*. But then I was quickly confronted with innumerable variations of sentences like:

> *It promises to be a good game, we plan to get there early.*

A colleague taught me what this was called. Knowing the name was somehow comforting; at least it gave me something to scrawl on papers. I have scrawled it many times: comma splices, like the Dude in *The Big Lebowski*, abide. There are variations over time, however, and one recent favorite is what I call the HCS (for "however comma splice"):

> *Steven Spielberg's recent films have been box-office disappointments, however his next release is expected to do well.*

The person was using *however* as a conjunction, more or less synonymous with *but*. For all I know, this will one day be acceptable, but it isn't now—and so it is entry II.B.4.d. in *How to Not Write Bad*.

I started seeing the HCS and a lot of other new bad-writing phenomena ten or twelve years ago. Surprise! That was about the time that online writing started to take off: going beyond e-mail to texts, blog posts, Facebook status updates, tweets, product comments, etc. In a lot of ways, this textual revolution is quite cool; for one thing, it's picked up many people by the napes of their necks and deposited them into the universe of writers. Certainly, it represents a huge positive change from the time not that long ago, when, other than a postcard here and there and the occasional thank-you note, most people didn't write much of anything at all. (Reports of letter writing in the pre-Internet era are greatly exaggerated.)

Nor do I agree with the complaint you'll find if you read more than a couple of op-ed pieces about the effect of this online culture on writing. That's the charge that smiley faces, "LOL"-type abbreviations, and terms like *diss* or *phat* are rampant in young people's prose. I think this is whack. (I realize all my attempts at slang are at least ten years out of date. My bad.) In fact, I don't remember encountering a single example in all my years of grading, except for a handful of ironic parries. Students realize that this kind of thing is in the wrong register for a college assignment.

But their writing does show an online influence in subtler ways. Writing for the computer is, for some reason, more like *talking* than writing for print is. That lends it a welcome freshness and naturalness. But there's a downside. Just as our spoken words disappear into the very air as soon as we utter then, it somehow seems that words on the computer screen aren't as *final* as they are on a piece of paper. One has a sense that the text is somehow provisional, that it will always be possible to make more changes. My friend and fellow teacher Devin Harner has said that something—a certain level of paying attention?—is lost when documents aren't *printed out.* I think he's on to something.

The general wordiness that characterizes so much writing today has got to be related to the incredible ease of using a keyboard to create shapely and professional-looking paragraphs. Back in the days when you had to scratch out each character with a quill pen (or even pound a manual typewriter), words were dearer and therefore were parceled out more judiciously. Now, after some stream-of-conscious keyboarding, you've got something that *looks* impressive. But it isn't. Paradoxically, it takes more effort to be concise than to be prolix, and people are (or think themselves to be) so pressed for time nowadays. As the philosopher Pascal once wisely wrote, "I would have written a shorter letter, but I did not have the time."

Don't worry about the ever-shifting sands of grammar and usage. Learning how to not write bad will, for one thing, attune your inner ear to these changes. Not-bad writing will help you hold on to your readers' attention, clearly communicate your meaning to them, and sometimes even convince them of your point of view. Without a doubt, it will serve to clarify your own thinking. And if you so desire, it will place you firmly on the road to writing *well*.

PART I

How to Not Write Bad: The One-Word Version

Read.

That one word refers to two things. The first is a big-picture deal: about the least quick of all possible fixes. But hear me out for a minute. Almost without exception, good writers read widely and frequently. By osmosis, they learn from the reading an incalculable amount about vocabulary, spelling, punctuation, style, rhythm, tone, and other crucial writing matters. They also pick up general random information, which also turns out to be important if you want to be a good, or even not-bad, writer.

Another college writing teacher, who calls himself "Professor X" and has written a book called *In the Basement of the Ivory Tower: Confessions of an Accidental Academic*, observes:

> I have come to think that the twist ingredients in the mysterious mix that makes a good writer may be (1)

> having read enough throughout a lifetime to have inter-
> nalized the rhythms of the written word, and (2) refin-
> ing the ability to mimic those rhythms.

He may be exaggerating the point. But he does have a point. Sometimes, when encountering an article or essay from a student who makes many spelling and punctuation mistakes, who uses words incorrectly, whose sentences meander in an awkward and ungainly fashion, I want to write on the paper: "Have read a lot!" Besides being a seriously weird tense (present perfect imperative?), that sentence represents a physical impossibility, outside of time-travel movies. So I don't write it. What I do try to tell all students is that if they want to be good writers, they should start reading as much as they can, starting now. And they should read all kinds of things.

Up until about ten years ago, I could leave it at that, maybe throwing in a great William Faulkner quote indicating that they need not confine themselves to the great works of Western litera-ture: "Read, read, read. Read everything—trash, classics, good and bad, and see how they do it. Just like a carpenter who works as an apprentice and studies the master. Read! You'll absorb it."

But things have changed. People nowadays read and write huge amounts of online stuff—texts, tweets, e-mails, blog posts, and so forth. As I mentioned in the introduction, I don't think there is anything especially wrong with this, and the composition end of it, at least, has led to a lot more people actually writing a lot more. But clearly, as far as reading goes, this online textuality doesn't have the Faulknerian effect. The material one is exposed to is too off-the-cuff and unilateral. For some reason, the stuff that helps your own writing has to have some measure of the traditional structure. It can be in print or online, can be any kind of book or any kind of article, but it seems to need to go through the old-fashioned pipeline. That is, selected and processed by an editor, and then "published."

How much reading will do the trick? The writer Malcolm Gladwell has popularized the notion that, in order to become an outstanding practitioner in any discipline, you need to devote to it roughly 10,000 hours of practice. I'll accept that in terms of reading. If you put in two hours a day, that works out to about thirteen and a half years. If you start when you're eight, you'll be done by college graduation!

The specific benefits of widespread reading are many. Certainly, it's the very best and most painless way to absorb the rules of the language. It's similar to table manners or conduct in public or any other social protocol—it's far more effective to learn by observing than by studying a textbook or being drilled in a classroom.

Prominent among the protocols of written language is spelling. And please, spare me the retort that spell-check programs mean we don't *have* to know how to spell anymore. No question, these applications can be helpful. If I happen to be writing about unfortunate digestive conditions, I can put down *diarrea* and then *diarhea* and finally *diarrhea*—getting a frisson of pleasure from seeing the last one absent a squiggly red line. But spell-check is anything but a cure-all and actually can make things worse. That is, it puts no red line under words that are correctly spelled, but are totally the *wrong* word. And thus the writer gets a false sense of security and hits save or send or print. This has produced a whole consortium of understandable errors like *he lead the way* (instead of *led*); *pouring over a book* (instead of *poring*); or *peaking his interest* (*piquing*), all of which will probably become the standard spelling some decades hence. (Just as the correct U.S. spelling changed years ago from *neighbour* and *colour* to the *u*-less versions.) More troubling are very common mistakes like confusing *your* and *you're*, *its* and *it's*, and *there* and *their*. And worst of all are the howlers that result when spell-check's suggestions are blindly taken. As I described in more detail in entry II.I.C.2., I have had students refer to wearing a *sequence-covered dress*, to *the Super Attendant of Schools*, to a *heroine attic*, and to an athlete who had to miss several weeks of the season because of *phenomena*, which baffled me till I realized it was supposed to be *pneumonia*.

Then there's punctuation, which once again, you learn far more thoroughly by reading widely than by studying. Not having read widely, most young writers today don't have a clue. Or, rather, they haven't mastered the rules, so are guided by intuition and/or sound, which are sometimes helpful but more often aren't. The intuition leads to the currently hugely popular "logical punctuation", which I have just used—it consists of putting periods and commas outside quotation marks, when the situation seems to call for it. This style has long been standard practice in the United Kingdom and various outposts of the British Empire, but not the United States. However, in the last five years or so, it's become inescapable on the Web—and in my classroom, despite repeated sardonic remarks from me that we are in Delaware, not Liverpool. On the logic that while this might be logical, and might become established sometime in the future, it is wrong now, I've begun to announce and enforce a one-point penalty on every assignment for infractions. In each class, a couple of (bright) students found this so irresistible that they kept on doing it till the end of the term. Go figure.

As for sound, students tend to insert commas at places where they would pause in speaking the sentence. This has about the same reliability as the rhythm method for birth control. In particular, it has led to the current vogue for commas after sentence-opening conjunctions. It works the other way as well. The majority of my students would write *Pittsburgh, Pennsylvania is his hometown*—leaving out the (required) comma after *Pennsylvania* because they *wouldn't* pause at that point in the sentence.

The benefits of reading extend far beyond protocol and rules. When you have read all kinds of (preferably good) prose by writers with diverse styles and approaches, your inner ear gets exposed to an amazing range of ways to perpetrate a sentence. They subtly but surely become part of your own repertoire. Trying to be a not-bad writer without having read your share of others' work is like trying to come up with a new theory in physics without having paid attention to the scientists that came before you, or writing a symphony without having listened to a lot of music. It's possible, I guess, but extremely difficult.

I quoted Faulkner earlier; now let me invoke some advice from his chief rival in twentieth-century American literature, Ernest Hemingway. In the book *Death in the Afternoon*, Hemingway counseled, "Write when there is something that you know; and not before; and not too damned much after." That has a nice ring to it, certainly more so than the clichéd motto of creative writing classes, "Write about what you know." But they both make the same basic point and they are both absolutely true. If Joe is a mediocre writer who knows his subject to the very depths of his soul (let's say his expertise is the qualities of a good video game), and Jane is an accomplished writer who's to a certain extent at sea (she's writing about the validity of the idea of global warming), Joe's essay is going to be stronger and better every time. Jane's will hem and haw and qualify and fudge, use passive voice and abstract nouns; it will circle around the subject to try to cover up all the gaps in her knowledge, and in so doing will just make the reader tired.

I imagine the write-what-you-know bromide is mocked because it implies, or seems to imply, that you're required to write about what you've *already* learned or experienced at the time you sit down at the keyboard: your childhood, your daydreams, your dog-walking routine, the layout of your bedroom, and so forth. But that isn't the case at all. Whatever your topic—and this is true of fiction as well as nonfiction—your writing will improve in direct proportion to the amount you read, research, investigate, and learn about it. I guarantee it.

There's a whole other aspect to the one-word solution for not writing bad. This one offers quite a contrast to the massive amount of time reading demands. Indeed, it's a pretty quick fix. The most effective *short-term* way to improve your writing is to read it aloud, sentence by sentence and word by word. There was a spoken language before there was a written language, and good writing has always been intimately connected to the ear, whether the short sentences of Hemingway or the near-endless periods of Samuel Johnson and David Foster Wallace.

Gustave Flaubert, renowned as one of the great all-time stylists, used what he called *la gueulade:* that is, "the shouting test." He would go out to an avenue of lime trees near his house and, yes, shout what he had written. It's the same principle as scrutinizing a photograph by blowing up its image on the computer screen; you really can identify the flaws.

Reading aloud isn't a panacea, even if you shout like Flaubert. At first, you may not catch the rum rhythms, the word repetition, the wordiness, the sentences that peter out with a whimper, not a bang. You need to develop your ear, just as a musician does. But eventually you'll start to really hear your sentences, and at some point you'll be able to shut up and listen with your *mind's* ear.

It'll give you good counsel, too. One of the favorite go-to rules of writing textbooks and teachers is to cut out the word *that* in sentences like *He told me that I needed to drop one class.* Improves the sentence, to be sure. But sometimes this is bad advice, for example, here: *Jack believed that Jill was a liar.* If you remove the *that,* you have *Jack believed Jill was a liar,* which a reader will find momentarily not only ambiguous but downright contradictory. That is, was Jack doubting Jill's truthfulness or accepting what she was saying? Even momentary reader confusion is bad, so *that* should stay. It's possible to come up with a rule for those situations, but the rule would be so complicated as to be nearly useless. (*Use the word* that *after a verb of expression or thought if the verb, in another connotation, can take a direct object.*) Much better to read it, hear it, and act accordingly.

Another example is word repetition, as in a sentence like *The last person to leave the room should examine the room for any possessions that were left behind.* If you've made your ear into a fine instrument, it will hear that second *room* as making a sound akin to fingernails on a chalkboard.

I talk a lot about "not-bad" writing. Another term for this is *the middle style*; sometimes it's claimed to be "transparent" prose. That's because it's clear, precise, and concise and doesn't call attention to itself, for good or ill. William Hazlitt gave it some other names, and a good characterization, back in 1821: "To write a genuine familiar or truly English style, is to write as any one would speak in common conversation, who had a thorough command and choice of words, or who could discourse with ease, force, and perspicuity." If you've ever seen a transcript of actual conversation, you know that you don't want to write *exactly* like that; too many false starts, too many *um*s, *ya know*s, and *like*s. Yet as Hazlitt recognized, not-bad writing is conversational to the core and reciting your work will help you master it.

Even *good* writing—such as the highly literary style of a Henry James, Vladimir Nabokov, or John Updike, or the irony of a Joan Didion or Sarah Vowell—reads aloud well. The worst of academic, bureaucratic, or legal prose doesn't; you have to take multiple breaths before you get to the end of a sentence, and the dull or vague or merely stiff wording just hits you over the head. It brings to mind what Harrison Ford supposedly said to George Lucas (always more of a visual than a word guy) on the set of *Star Wars*: "You can write this shit, George, but you sure can't say it."

A word you see a lot nowadays is *mindfulness*. I confess I don't know exactly what it means; something having to do with meditation and/or yoga, I believe. But the concept can definitely, and profitably, be adapted to writing. The opposite of mindful writing is careless, unexamined, unattended-to prose: what Truman Capote may have had in mind when he said (referring to Beat Generation authors), "That isn't writing at all, it's typing." Mindless writing is a data dump and one sees it far too often nowadays.

I hope I don't sound like the "Get off my lawn!" guy too often in this book, but I'll briefly embrace this persona for a rant about multitasking, that is, the predilection of youth (broadly defined) to do several things at once, most or all of them electronic. Much attention, research, and verbiage has been devoted to this subject, and I freely confess that I haven't studied the accumulated wisdom and thus am not an expert. However. I am convinced that multitasking—either the act itself or a multitasking state of mind—promotes the mindless writing I am confronted with every day. Without a doubt, if you have several things going on at once, you are perfectly capable of expressing an idea along the lines of *Dude, where should we eat?* or *OMG, did you see what she's wearing?* But anything more complicated than that—and anything you would want to write for a broader public is more complicated than that—well, it just can't be done.

In other words, I would bet a lot of money that the student who wrote the following sentence had several other things going on:

Not only do journalists possess an undying passion to uncover and showcase relevant information to enhance the public's knowledge on current events, but exhibit a willingness to go to great lengths to obtain stories fit to print.

It has all the telltale signs of mindless writing: wordiness, clichés, and catchphrases poorly used; subjects and verbs that don't line up; incorrect use of words; faulty parallelism. It might not be a bad idea to copy it down and put it up on your bulletin board as an example of what not to do. And make no mistake: merely listening to music while trying to write constitutes multitasking, not to mention texting, watching TV, scanning a computer, and so forth. Any of these things takes the necessary attention away from the task at hand. So if you don't want to write badly, don't do them.

A big part of mindful writing is an awareness of and attentiveness to the (hypothetical or actual) person who will eventually be reading your words. Ideally, you look him or her in the eye, as it were. You note a spark of interest or a puzzled look or the glazed expression that indicates incipient boredom, and respond accordingly. Few of us are lucky enough to have a real live person ready and willing to hear our stuff. But that's okay. Cooking a stew, you don't need an outside opinion; you just take a taste now and again. It's the same with writing. Reading aloud—literally or figuratively—will help you take one step away from your work and single-handedly become what Robert Graves called "the reader over your shoulder."

So read.

PART II

How to Not Write Wrong

Note: In Parts II and III, examples of what *not* to do will be ~~crossed out~~ or [set in brackets].

A. The Elements of House Style

Which is correct, *6 PM, 6 P.M.,* or *6 p.m.*?

The answer is, all of them!—and I apologize for starting off this part of the book with a trick question. This is an issue of *style* in the sense of *The AP Stylebook* and MLA Style—basically, a set of rules and conventions having to do with abbreviation, capitalization, and so forth that is followed by a particular publication or organization. If your professor, company, or publication subscribes to a certain house style, follow it. If not, the most important thing is to be consistent. That is, if on page 1 you write *6 p.m.,* spell out the number *fifteen*, and put "Gone with the Wind" in quotation marks, make sure you do things the same way all through your text.

1. NUMBERS AND ABBREVIATIONS

That said, not-bad writers tend to follow some general style guidelines. Most prominently, they try to stay away if at all possible from numerals, abbreviations, capitalization, and symbols like &, %, #, +, >, /, and @. The underlying reason for this has to do with the whole read-aloud thing. In reciting the sentence below, for example, you wouldn't say "St." or "Dr."; and *fourteen* just reads more fluently than *14*.

> [*The Dr. has had his office @ #321 Livingston St. for >20 years.*]

It's better to write it as you would say it:

> *The doctor has had his office at 321 Livingston Street for more than twenty years.* (Street addresses are always given in numerals, hence the *321*.)

As for state names, never abbreviate when they're four letters or less, or when they're standing alone.

> *He hails from ~~Calif.~~ California.*

It isn't wrong or necessarily bad to abbreviate a state name when it immediately follows a city, but note that the Associated Press stopped doing this in 2010. That is, the AP now refers to *Albany, New York,* not *Albany, N.Y.*

It's similar with months. Always spell out the months from March through July. For the rest, spell out when alone (*I was born in February*); when it's followed by the day, abbreviation is okay, as long as you're consistent (*I was born on Feb. 22*).

Of course, it would look silly to spell out terms customarily given by abbreviations, initials, or acronyms—to write, that is:

> [*The band played a song from its new compact disk on Mister David Letterman's talk show, which airs on the Columbia Broadcasting System.*]

> *The band played a song from its new CD on David Letterman's CBS talk show.*

Long-established custom dictates that numbers above 100, sports scores, dates, temperatures, ratios, betting odds, prices, street addresses, phone numbers, and generally stuff referring to numbers as numbers be presented in numerals rather than words.

> *The Yankees beat the Red Sox yesterday by a score of 5–2. The two teams have met 223 times; the Yankees lead, 130–93.*

Otherwise, you won't go wrong if you follow a simple principle: when in doubt, spell it out.

2. CAPITALIZATION

A similar strategy goes for capital letters. They're called on, most frequently, to indicate proper nouns, which are, generally speaking, the official names of people, places, trade names, and organizations. For example: *General Electric, the University of Southern California, the Atlantic Ocean, the Rolling Stones, Mars, Albany, John Glenn, Excedrin,* and *France.* (But not *my Wife, the Ocean, an Antibiotic,* or *the Supermarket.*)

Titles and honorifics that come *before* a name are also capitalized; *Mr., Mrs., Miss, Ms.,* and *Dr.* are abbreviated as well. But if you are merely giving a description of the person or naming his or her job—even before the name—use lowercase.

> *The panelists will be lawyer Mike Jones, anchorwoman Claudia Axelrod, and President Barack Obama.*

After a name, even titles are lowercased:

> *Barack Obama is the president, Benedict is the pope, and Harvey Weill is the district attorney.*

Seasons, directions, and relatives (for some reason, the three most commonly wrongly capitalized categories) are rendered in lowercase as well:

> [*Every Summer, my Mother and Father and I got in the car and drove West.*]

Every summer, my mother and father and I got in the car and drove west.

3. ITALICS

A surprising number of people don't realize that, in a text, italics or underlining indicate exactly the same thing. In typewriter days, it wasn't possible to indicate italics, so we underlined for emphasis. Now that everybody writes on computers, underlining isn't necessary, so don't do it. Use italics, but only for emphasis, for titles of books and other compositions (as long as you're consistent), to indicate words as words (as is done throughout this book), and for words in languages other than English. Putting a word in all capital letters is not an acceptable way to indicate any of these things, except in dialogue, where all-caps can suggest shouting at a very high volume, or, occasionally, in informal writing, where it can be amusing.

The foreign-language item demands some amplification. If a foreign word is familiar enough that readers will understand what it means—think joie de vivre, siesta, zeitgeist, espresso—don't italicize it. However, sometimes you may have reason to use a more obscure foreign word or a short quotation from something said or written in a foreign language. Italicize the word or quote—and make sure you quickly translate it.

One complication with italics is e-mail. Some e-mail programs allow italicization, but others play dumb when you hit the appropriate keys, or instead give you a Spanish tilde sign or some other odd piece of punctuation. Some people compensate for this by using special cues for emphasis, like *this* or _this_ That's okay for e-mail, but stay away for it in any other setting.

4. THERE IS NO REASON EVER TO USE BOLDFACE IN A PIECE OF WRITING, EXCEPT FOR A SECTION HEADING (LIKE THIS)

Students commonly use bold instead of the proper typographical way to indicate emphasis or a title, which is italics. Aside from being counter to standard usage, it's jarring; each boldfaced word makes the reader jump.

[*Why do they insist on putting* **Hamlet** *in bold?*]

Why do they insist on putting Hamlet *in bold?*

B. Punctuation

1. '

a. ~~Plurality's~~ Pluralities

Punctuation isn't sexy, but it's actually a key to not-bad writing. That's because of the concept I discussed at the end of the last chapter, "mindful writing." You can dismiss apostrophes—and punctuation in general—as just a series of technical details. I prefer to look at them as measures of mindfulness. When you write carelessly or automatically—mind*less*ly, that is—the chances of apostrophizing correctly are pretty slim. They steadily improve as you begin to pay attention.

An easy thing to remember is not to use apostrophes—ever—to

indicate a plural, no matter how tempting it seems. Doing so will get you pilloried in a book like *Eats, Shoots & Leaves*.

> [*They have three TV's on the first floor and four on the second, so if you don't like what's on, you can just walk into another room!*]

Should be *TVs*, just as it should be *IOUs*, *SUVs*, and *C.D.s*. (The first two examples don't have periods between the capital letters; the third does. That's a matter of house style and will vary by publication. The rule about no apostrophe before the *s* is the same in either case.)

The same goes for decades and centuries, which are in fact plurals (an accumulation of ten years for a decade, 100 for a century). Some publications countenance *the 1800's* or *the 60's*, but it's wrong. The *1960s*, *the '60s*, and *the sixties* are all okay, as long as you're consistent.

A small number of students instinctively and wrongly reach for the apostrophe to indicate the plural of a *y*-ending word: *several country's* instead of *several countries*. The move is a bit more understandable with proper nouns, but equally incorrect. That is, the correct forms are:

> *Six Kennedys attended the ceremony.*

and

> *Over his career he's won seventeen Grammys.*

Other writers mess up by pluralizing *y*-ending words when the intention is merely to indicate a possessive:

> [*When the mom took away the babies' pacifier, he started crying.*]

> *When the mom took away the baby's pacifier, he started crying.*

And that brings us to the next topic.

b. Possessed

The basic form of possessive apostrophes is *blank's thingamajig*, where both words are nouns and *thingamajig* belongs to or is associated with *blank*. Another way to look at it is that an apostrophe is called for if you can change the wording to *the thingamajig of blank*. This is incredibly common in speaking, writing, and singing, as exemplified in the songs "Mickey's Monkey," "Judy's Turn to Cry," and "John Brown's Body."

The basic form is easy enough. It can get a little trickier when you're indicating a possessive of a noun ending with the letter *s*. Here's a two-step way to deal with it. (1) An apostrophe always follows the *s*. (2) If the word is a singular, or a proper name, you put another *s* after the apostrophe. If not, you do not.

> *Phyllis's dress's zipper is broken.*

However (and this is step 3), if the word is a plural, most style guides have you leave out the second *s*, on the theory, I guess, that it's not pronounced.

The first half of the twins' birthday party is being held at the Smiths' house and the second part at the Joneses'.

That example brings two further guidelines to mind. First, the plural of *Jones* is indeed *Joneses*. Most *s*-ending common and proper nouns follow an add *-es* form; the most common exception is *series*, the plural of which is *series*. Second, if you want to put a sign outside your house—a questionable idea to begin with—inscribe the plural of your name followed by an apostrophe, that is, *The Yagodas'*; "house" or "place" is understood. An apostrophe-less *The Yagodas* just makes it seem like a verb is missing. And *The Yagoda's* makes no sense, except in reference to the domicile of a person who refers to himself as "The Yagoda."

A final apostrophe issue is where (if anywhere) it's placed in formulations like *Farmers Market, Boys Club,* and *Stockholders Meeting.*

I confess that I find this a toughie. What helps clear it up for me is pretending that the first word in the phrase is *men*—or *women* or *children* or any plural that doesn't end in *s*. You would never write *men room, men department,* or *men club,* and you obviously shouldn't write *mens room, mens department,* etc. (because there is no such word as *mens*). Instead, the correct forms would be *men's room, men's department,* and *men's club.* It works out that almost always the apostrophe should follow the *s*. And the above examples should be *Farmers' Market, Boys' Club,* and *Stockholders' Meeting.* In fact, in phrases like this, the apostrophe should almost always follow the *s*. (The exception, such as *farmer's tan, Mother's Day,* or, speaking of songs, *"It's a Man's World,"* comes where the reference is to the prototypical singular farmer, mom, or man.)

c. This Should Not Be Necessary, but . . .

Do not write *your* (possessive of *you*) instead of *you're* (contraction of *you are*) or *it's* (contraction of *it is*) instead of *its* (possessive of *it*), or vice versa. If you do, it looks very bad and you will be mocked. Spell-check will not help you out. You just need to be mindful.

d. An Incredibly Geeky Point

In typewriter days, the keyboard provided a single vertical mark to indicate apostrophe, opening single quote, and closing single quote. But in a published text, these are not the same. The apostrophe and the closing single quote are the same and look like this: '. The opening single quote looks like this: '.

This was no problem back then: if a typewritten (or handwritten) text was going to be published, typesetters would take care of sorting out the apostrophes and single quotes. The trouble came with the arrival of word processing programs. Computer keyboards also have a single key for those three symbols, but the programs offer print-style fonts and think they are smart enough to figure out which symbol you want in a particular situation. That's not always the case, however. Consider the following sentence, which I let Microsoft Word have its way with:

[*Rock 'n' roll was very big in the '60s.*]

There should be an apostrophe before *n* and *60s*, to indicate stuff that is left out, the same way the apostrophe works in contractions like *can't* or *I'm*. Instead, there is an opening single quote.

I admitted this was a geeky point, and the fact is that 99 percent of people, or more, won't notice the problem. But to me it counts as bad writing. If you agree and want to correct the error, there are various workarounds. The one I use is to trick the program by typing a second apostrophe after the incorrect one:

> [*Rock "n' roll was very big in the "60s.*]

Then if you delete the incorrect one, you will be left with true apostrophes:

> *Rock 'n' roll was very big in the '60s.*

2. **-**

Hyphenation can cause vexation. It certainly did in one of my students, who handed in an article containing this sentence:

> [*Our day began with a run down of the up-coming shark cage diving experience.*]

At three points in the sentence, he had to make one of three choices: separate words, hyphenated phrase, or one word. He made a wrong choice every time. *Rundown* and *upcoming* may have been separate or hyphenated at one time in the history of the English language (that's generally the way phrases evolve over time—*base ball* to *base-ball* to *baseball*), but now they're one word. How are you supposed to know that? Well, the more you read, the more you get a feel for it. But leaving that aside, there's a simple answer:

LOOK THEM UP IN THE DICTIONARY! Do the same for words formed with prefixes like *un*, *self*, *ex*, *all*, *de*, *non*, and *re*.

That sounds a little easier than it is and brings up a conundrum I think of as the Blind Spot Problem. It derives from the notion of the vehicular blind spot—the idea that, while driving, you cannot see some areas of the road through your rearview or side mirrors or by looking due left or due right, and thus you have to turn around to see if it's okay to change lanes, a risky move at high speeds.

If you are puzzled or unsure about a particular issue of spelling, punctuation, or grammar (a known unknown), there is help to be had in various kinds of online and print resources. But what if you aren't aware that you aren't aware of how it's supposed to be done? That's the Blind Spot Problem (BSP for short). Where it presents the biggest problem, nowadays, is the general issue of word separation. There seems to be a widespread desire to take compound words that have been recognized as such for decades, sometimes centuries, and take them apart again. I have read countless assignments with such phrases as:

Work place

Long time (adjective)

Life time

Fire works

Weather man

Mean time

Some times

Touch down (in *foot ball;* I mean, *football*)

Under ground (adjective)

So how do you defeat the blind spot and *realize* that you don't know? My best answer is the equivalent of craning your neck in a car. (Fortunately, this is totally safe at your desk or in the library.) That is, teach yourself that there is a category of unknowns having to do with the question of one word, two words, or a hyphenation. Learn to recognize the situations where the question arises, and that the trend of the English language over time is toward one-word compounds. If you have to make a choice—let's say you want to refer to an *underground, under-ground,* or *under ground* bunker—and if you are anything less than 100 percent certain which one it should be, look it up, in a dictionary or on a reliable Web site.

The first couple of dozen times, your neck will probably feel pretty sore from all that virtual craning. But after time you'll get a sense of the way the rules work, and you can cruise along

Speaking of the rules, let's get back to my student who referred to a *shark cage diving experience.* He couldn't have looked that up, since the dictionary doesn't have an entry for it, but he shouldn't have had to. *Shark cage diving* is a compound adjective—that is, a phrase, made up of two or more words, that modifies a noun—and compound adjectives before a noun (*experience*) get hyphenated:

my shark-cage-diving experience

any school-age children

some out-of-date and messed-up ideas

a seven-year-old boy

the happy-face button

*an I-just-ate-something-that-really-disagreed-with-me
    expression*

There are three notable situations where a compound adjective is *not* hyphenated. The first is when the modifying phrase consists of all adjectives or an adverb followed by an adjective. For example, *A standard yellow school bus is a remarkably attractive vehicle.* Second, you don't hyphenate proper nouns or extremely familiar two-word phrases. Thus, *Our high school graduation was held in the Yankee Stadium parking lot.* (One exception to this is the quaintly named institution The New-York Historical Society, a classic test for copyeditors.) And finally, the hyphens are usually dispensed with when the compound phrase stands alone—that is, does not precede a noun:

[*The boy is seven-years-old, the ideas are out-of-date, and I am fed-up.*]

The boy is seven years old, the ideas are out of date, and I am fed up.

Finally, please note that it's never correct to put space before a hyphen (except in very rare cases, like a reference to "the suffix *–less*") It's correct to put space *after* a hyphen in only one situation, of which this is an example:

>*This year Rollins had 17- and 28-game hitting streaks.*

3. —

A dash—sometimes known as an "em-dash"—is created when you type two hyphens in a row. (Your word processing program, as if by magic, will make them into one solid line.) Do not put a space before or after the dash.

>[*I hate one day of the week- Monday.*]

>[*I hate one day of the week - Monday.*]

>[*I hate one day of the week - - Monday.*]

>*I hate one day of the week—Monday.*

Don't put any other punctuation before or after a dash, even if doing so seems to make sense. This was customary in the nineteenth century and before. It is not now.

>[*The vice president asked for a pay raise—his first in seven years—,never thinking the media would hear about it.*]

The vice president asked for a pay raise—his first in seven years—never thinking the media would hear about it.

Finally, limit your dashes. The maximum is one per sentence (if you're using it as a colon substitute) or two (if you're using them in place of parentheses.). Beyond that lies confusion.

[*He accumulated one college degree—from Michigan State—and two PhDs—from Harvard and NYU—before his thirtieth birthday.*]

He accumulated one college degree (from Michigan State) and two PhDs (from Harvard and NYU) before his thirtieth birthday.

4. ,

a. Identification Crisis

Commas yield the most errors of any category of punctuation, and their use in identification yields the highest percentage of comma errors. When a poor or mindless writer is at the keyboard, you can be pretty certain he or she will get this wrong. Getting it right is a matter of studying the rules, some mindful focus, and practicing hearing-with-your-mind's-ear writing. Anyway, if you can master this entry, you will have taken several big and important steps in the right direction.

Take a look at this sentence:

[*I went to see the movie,* True Grit *with my friend, Bill.*]

It's very common to put a comma after *movie* and *friend*—
and sometimes after *Grit*—in examples such as this. But doing
so is wrong—unless *True Grit* is the only movie in the world and Bill
is the speaker's only friend.

The first is definitely not the case, and you can be fairly confident the second isn't, either. Therefore, the correct form is:

> *I went to see the movie* True Grit *with my friend Bill.*

If that seems funky or weird or anything short of clearly right,
bear with me a minute and take a look at another correct sentence.

> *I went to see the Coen brothers' latest movie,* True Grit,
> *with my oldest friend, Bill.*

You need a comma after *movie* because *True Grit* and only *True
Grit* is the brothers' latest film, and after *Bill* because he and only
he is the speaker's oldest friend. (For why you need one after *Grit*,
see the next entry.)

The structure we're talking about is *identifier-noun*. The general rule is that if the noun is *not* the only thing in the world described by the identifier, leave out the comma. But if the identifier
describes that noun and that noun alone, the comma is required.

There is one exception. If the identifier is preceded by *a*, *an*, a
number, or a quantifying phrase like *a couple of*, use a comma before and after the noun.

> *A local merchant, Bob Hamilton, has opened his second
> Taco Bell.*

> *Two members of the Hall of Fame, Johnny Bench and Willie Mays, will give speeches at the event.*

With *the* or a possessive before the identifier, the basic rule applies. That is, use a comma if the identifier describes a unique person or thing:

> *The president of the Springfield Bar Association, Harold Cullen, was reelected unanimously.*

> *My son, John, is awesome. (If you have just one son.)*

But withhold the comma if not unique:

> *My son John is awesome. (If you have more than one son.)*

> *The artist David Hockney is a master of color.*

> [*I love the cellist, Yo-Yo Ma.*]

If nothing comes before the identification, don't use a comma; the word *the* is implied.

> [*The keynote speech was given by attorney, Harold Cullen.*]

> *The keynote speech was given by attorney Harold Cullen.*

No one seems to have a problem with the idea that if the identification comes *after* the noun, it should always be surrounded by commas:

> *Harold Meyerson, a local merchant, gave the keynote address.*

However, students often wrongly omit a *the* or *a* in sentences of this type:

> [*Jill Meyers, sophomore, is president of the sorority.*]

> *Jill Meyers, a sophomore, is president of the sorority.*

> [*The U.S. was represented by Hillary Clinton, secretary of state.*]

> *The U.S. was represented by Hillary Clinton, the secretary of state.*

Sometimes the identifier consists of *the, a,* or a possessive followed by two or more adjectives. In some cases, a comma goes between the adjectives, and in some cases not.

> a. [*In my safe I have a valuable, wooden nickel.*]

> b. *In my safe I have a valuable wooden nickel.*

a. [*The best fruit of all is a ripe juicy flavorful peach.*]

b. *The best fruit of all is a ripe, juicy, flavorful peach.*

Why is *a* wrong and *b* right, and how can you decide whether to use commas in these situations? The rule I learned in junior high school still holds. Anytime you can insert the word *and* between adjectives and it still sounds fine, use a comma. If not, don't.

b. The Case(s) of the Missing Comma

i. A related issue is the epidemic of missing commas after parenthetical phrases or appositives—that is, self-enclosed material that's within a sentence, but not essential to its meaning.

[*My father, who gave new meaning to the expression* hardworking *never took a vacation.*]

My father, who gave new meaning to the expression hardworking, *never took a vacation.*

———————

[*He was born in Des Moines, Iowa in 1964.*]

He was born in Des Moines, Iowa, in 1964.

———————

[*Philip Roth, author of* Portnoy's Complaint *and many other books is a perennial contender for the Nobel Prize.*]

Philip Roth, author of Portnoy's Complaint *and many other books, is a perennial contender for the Nobel Prize.*

I'm not sure why this mistake is so tempting. It may sometimes be because these phrases are so long that by the time we get to the end of them, we've forgotten about the first comma. In any case, a strategy to prevent it is to remember the acronym ICE. That is, whenever you find yourself using a comma to precede an *Identification*, *Characterization*, or *Explanation*, remember that the ICE *has* to be followed by a second comma. (The exception is when the ICE ends the sentence, in which case it's followed by a period.)

ii. Students also commonly leave out the comma after a modifying phrase or dependent clause.

[*By instituting all these new rules so soon after the start of the semester the university is creating chaos.*]

By instituting all these new rules so soon after the start of the semester, the university is creating chaos.

———————

[*When the time is right to introduce a campaign the public relations department will get busy.*]

When the time is right to introduce a campaign, the public relations department will get busy.

Note that this rule holds even when the modifying phrase or clause doesn't start out the sentence.

> [*Carson tried to slip into the conference unnoticed, but since he was wearing a blindingly white suit that didn't happen.*]

> *Carson tried to slip into the conference unnoticed, but since he was wearing a blindingly white suit, that didn't happen.**

You can't go wrong in using a comma after a modifying phrase or dependent clause. However, in the case of a very short phrase—three words or less, and especially in the case of time elements—it can be okay or even preferable to leave the comma out.

> *Tomorrow I'll be home.*

> *Nowadays people leave out commas when they can get away with it.*

But note that even with a short intro, a comma is often needed to avoid ambiguity. Scrutinize the sentence to find out.

> [*However last night's performance was a triumph.*]

> *However, last night's performance was a triumph.*

---

* Sticklers will put a comma after the *but* in that sentence. See the next footnote.

[*Despite the law students tailgated in greater numbers than last year.*]

Is the writer talking about law students? No. So:

Despite the law, students tailgated in greater numbers than last year.

iii. When a sentence consists of two or more independent clauses (groups of words that can stand on their own as a sentence) joined by a conjunction, such as *and* or *but*, put a comma before (but not after) the conjunction

[*I waited in the terminal for two and a half hours but the bus never came.*]

I waited in the terminal for two and a half hours, but the bus never came.

As in section **ii.**, the comma can sometimes be omitted when the clauses are very short (and there's no confusion or ambiguity). But you can never go wrong in using it.

She likes me but I like her roommate.

She likes me, but I like her roommate.

c. But, a Comma *Feels* Right!

Roughly at the beginning of the twenty-first century, I began to see a lot of sentences like:

[*But, I don't agree.*]

And:

[*And, using a comma this way is weirdly popular.*]

By now, students put a comma in that spot more often than they don't. Commas after sentence-starting *But*s, *And*s, and *Yet*s have even started to show up in Associated Press dispatches and *New York Times* articles, as well as in blogs and other writing on the Web. I think people use commas in this spot to mimic the pause they might insert when speaking such sentences. But for the last 150 years or so, punctuation rules have been based on grammar, not sound. And so a comma here is wrong.*

More generally, students seem to reach for a comma whenever they feel any anxiety about a sentence's syntax, when they find

---

* That's not to say that sound is never a factor in comma use. In many situations, a comma is optional, and the rhythm of the sentence is an important factor in deciding whether to use one. For example, if a sentence-opening conjunction is followed by a parenthetical phrase, you may (but aren't required to) use a comma after the conjunction. *But, as far as vacations go, my whole family prefers the beach.* In this case, it makes sense to choose based on whether you hear a pause after *But.*

themselves using an unfamiliar word, to separate a long noun phrase from a verb or a long adjective phrase from a noun, or just when they feel a pause coming on:

[*Approximately, fifteen percent of the class are minority group members.*]

[*Everyone who signed the petition, was disciplined.*]

[*Smith described the concert as, "a blast."*]

[*He shares a house with three, senior, premed students.*]

[*Megan washed the dishes, and, wiped the counter.*]

All the commas in all those sentences need to go. As with all punctuation, the general trend over time is "Less is more." A good strategy for commas is, if you can't name a specific reason why it needs to be there, leave it out.

d. Splice Girls . . . and Boys

Comma splice is a term for the linking of two independent clauses (that is, grammatical units that contain a subject and a verb and could stand alone as sentences) with a comma instead of a semicolon, period, or conjunction. As I noted in the introduction, when I started teaching I was gobsmacked by the multitude of comma splices that confronted me. They have not abated.

> [*He used to be a moderate, now he's a card-carrying Occupy Wall Street type.*]

> *He used to be a moderate. Now he's a card-carrying Occupy Wall Street type.*

> *He used to be a moderate; now he's a card-carrying Occupy Wall Street type.*

> *He used to be a moderate, but now he's a card-carrying Occupy Wall Street type.*

The second, third, and fourth examples are equally correct. You make your choice by, you got it, reading aloud and picking the one that best suits the context, your style, and your ear. Here, I would go with the semicolon. How about you?

Be careful of the word *however*. A recent trend is to use it as a conjunction (sort of a fancier version of *but*); down that road lie commas splices, and trouble.

> [*Tuition will go up again next year, however, it will be the smallest increase in five years.*]

> *Tuition will go up again next year. However, it will be the smallest increase in five years.*

> *Tuition will go up again next year, but it will be the smallest increase in five years.*

Comma splices are okay in rare cases, including sentences where even a semicolon would slow things down too much:

I talked to John, John talked to Lisa.

e. The Oxford Comma

In a series of three or more items, do you put a comma after the penultimate one (right before the *and* or *or*)? That's another trick question. If you are writing for the Associated Press, the answer is no. If you are writing for the *New Yorker* or the Oxford University Press, the answer is yes. (The OUP is so well known for this protocol that it has come to be referred to as "the Oxford comma.") If you're writing for yourself, the key thing—as in style choices generally—is consistency: choose a style you like, and stick with it.

We brought wine, cheese and snacks to the party.

We brought wine, cheese, and snacks to the party.

That said, in order to prevent ambiguity, you sometimes need to use the Oxford comma.

The greatest singing duos in history are Simon and Garfunkel, Jan and Dean, and Brooks and Dunn.

I am thankful for my parents, Ayn Rand, and God.

The OC is also called for when the items in the list are independent clauses or are long.

> *Bill washed up, I took a shower, and we all went to sleep.*

> *For furnishing his dorm room, he brought all his Boy Scout ribbons, the home-run ball Chase Utley personally autographed for him in 2007, and a refrigerator his mother picked out for him at Target.*

5. ;

My initial thought is to limit this entry to one sentence: "If you feel like using a semicolon, lie down until the urge goes away."

That is because when my students utilize this piece of punctuation, a substantial majority of them utilize it incorrectly. Just this past semester, a student's article for a feature writing class had this: *The Delaware Welcome Visitors Center is a sight for sore eyes; literally.* What she needed was a dash or a colon—pieces of punctuation I have already employed three times in this entry. (For the other problems in the sentence, see "Apostrophe" and "*Literally.*")

But while it is tempting to outlaw semicolons and just move on, that would be too easy. For one thing, there is a particular circumstance when a semicolon absolutely has to be used. This is a series of three or more items, one or more of which contain a comma. Thus:

> *I've lived in Madison, Wisconsin; Wilmington, Delaware; and Toledo, Ohio.*

You can see the confusion that would result if the semicolons were replaced by commas, or nothing. A semicolon is called for in only one other situation, and it really isn't that hard to grasp. A semicolon can be used to connect two independent clauses if the clauses aren't already linked by conjunctions (*and, but, although,* etc.).* This can be quite useful if the clauses are short, and a period would create an unintended Hemingway or See-Dick-Run sound:

> *I got home last night; Bill was already there.*

A colon or dash could also be employed in such sentences, but these marks imply an "and therefore" or an "and here's what I mean" connection between the two elements. A semicolon suggests a relationship as well, but a more subtle or complicated one.

> *John Updike wrote sixty-three books; I wonder how he found time to sleep.*
>
> *I really like Sauvignon Blanc; Chardonnay is too oaky for my tastes.*

Just remember: use this piece of punctuation in a series whose elements have commas, or a sentence consisting of two complete sentences. Otherwise, step away from the semicolon.

---

* If you're going for an old-fashioned, Henry James kind of thing, you can use a semicolon before an *and, but, yet,* or *for.*

> *Congress voted to fund twenty-seven pork-barrel projects this term; but the president had other things in mind.*

6. :

The colon presents two issues of correctness. The first is simple: do not use more than one of them in a sentence or you will seriously confuse the reader.

The second concerns capitalization after a colon. If what follows isn't a complete sentence, do not capitalize (unless the first word is a proper noun).

> *The president listed three economic goals: lower taxes, increased trade and more jobs.*

If what follows the colon *is* a complete sentence, follow house style; if there is no house style, follow your own lights, but be consistent.

> *I follow a simple principle: To thine own self be true.*

> *I follow a simple principle: to thine own self be true.*

7. " "

a. Doubling Down

With two exceptions, in the United States one always uses double quotation marks ("like this") rather than the single quotes, or "inverted commas," favored in the United Kingdom and the former and current outposts of the British Empire ('like this'). Seems simple enough, but recently students have grown unaccountably fond of using single quotes, not so much for actual quotations but for ironic scare quotes and one- or two-word catchphrases. (Using quotation marks for anything other than quoting what someone said or wrote, or in rendering titles of books or movies and the like, is usually a bad idea stylistically, but that's a topic for Part III). So:

[*We're devoting Friday to some serious 'day drinking.'*]

We're devoting Friday to some serious "day drinking."

The two exceptions: single quotes are properly used in the United States in newspaper headlines—such as FORD TO CITY: 'DROP DEAD'—and in quotes within quotes:

"When I walked in at three in the morning," he said, "my mom was like, 'You're grounded.'"

b. Go Inside

[*Tonight we're seeing "My Fair Lady".*]

[*"I feel like going to the beach this weekend", he said.*]

Students and other people seem to find it irresistible these days to place periods and commas outside quotation marks. And why shouldn't they? The stuff inside the quote marks is a unit, and thus it would appear logical to put punctuation outside it. Indeed, doing so is correct, assuming that you live in the British Isles. But in America, we never put commas or periods outside quotation marks. And so this is an easy one to remember. Never outside, always inside.

> *Tonight we're seeing "My Fair Lady."*

> *"I feel like going to the beach this weekend," he said.*

Bear in mind that this applies only to periods and commas. We in the United States are fine with putting every *other* kind of punctuation outside of quotation marks unless the punctuation is part of the quote. Indeed, I think I can say without fear of contradiction that semicolons and colons *never* go inside quotation marks.

I am so excited to be singing Rodgers and Hart's "Have You Met Miss Jones?"!

Bob's favorite word is "chillax"; isn't yours "ginormous"?

8. ( )

There are three relevant rules for parentheses themselves:

1. If you set down an open one (with the outside of the curve facing left), you have to eventually set down a closed one, with the outside of the curve facing right. (Don't laugh—I have encountered such orphan parentheses on lots of occasions.)

2. You can't follow a set of parentheses immediately with another set of parentheses, unless you're being cute. Being cute is a risky game.

3. If by any chance you feel you need to use a pair of parentheses within a pair of parentheses, first of all, see if there is a way to avoid this. If there isn't, use brackets ([]) instead of parentheses for the interior pair. That reminds me that the only other common use for brackets is to briefly clarify something ambiguous or deleted within a quotation.

> *When Haldeman said that John Dean was about to testify, Nixon replied, "That's a load of [expletive deleted]."*

The content *inside* parentheses (TCIP) has to conform to a lot of rules, many of them relating to the relationship between the TCIP and the material that comes before it. If both are complete sentences (and remember that TCIP can be more than one sentence), follow this pattern.

> *I loved the play last night. (The rest of the audience seemed to feel otherwise. Or so it seemed.)*

If TCIP is not a complete sentence, then:

1. Do not put any punctuation immediately before or after the open parenthesis.

2. Make the first word of TCIP lowercase, unless a proper noun.

3. No punctuation right before the close parenthesis, with the occasional exception, in informal writing, of an exclamation point or question mark.

4. Choose whether or not to use any punctuation after the close parenthesis based on the particular needs of the sentence.

Here are some examples, all of them in the form of song titles (parenthetical song titles being a splendid and underappreciated genre). The titles are given in lowercase so as to show proper capitalization, and closing punctuation is included.

> *(You gotta) fight for your right (to party).*
>
> *There's a kind of hush (all over the world).*
>
> *You can look (but you better not touch).*
>
> *I (who have nothing).*
>
> *Don't come home a drinkin' (with lovin' on your mind).*
>
> *Alone again (naturally).*
>
> *If I said you had a beautiful body (would you hold it against me)?*

What about punctuation when the parentheses come in the middle of sentence? Simply act as though the parens were not there, and put the appropriate punctuation at the end of the close parenthesis. (This is the opposite of what you do with em-dashes. Go figure.)

> *Weighing in on the question were Bernstein (against it), Gallo (for it), and Allenson (undecided).*

C. Words

1. THE SINGLE MOST COMMON MISTAKE IS THE MOST EASILY FIXABLE MISTAKE

Simply put, this is to clean up after yourself. Writing on computers leads to a category of sloppy error that was rare in typewriter days and probably nonexistent when people used pen on paper: forgetting to delete a word.

> [*The president announced an initiative that ~~would~~ will create a new academic department.*]

"Policing the area," as it were, is an aspect of attentiveness or mindfulness, and it's not hard to do. So do it.

2. SPELLING

a. Homophone-phobia

Spell-check programs are great. Spell-check programs are a disaster.

Let me explain.

Back in the old days, students would frequently make spelling mistakes like *embarass* (instead of *embarrass*) or *influencial* (instead of *influential*). No more. Modern word processing programs put squiggly red lines under misspelled words or, better yet, silently correct them (as mine just tried to do with *embarass*).

The programs are not perfect, even on their own terms. My version of Microsoft Word accepts *miniscule* unsquiggled, even though the correct spelling is *minuscule*, and *alright* even though *all right* is preferred by every authority I'm aware of. And although Word does in fact indicate that *momento* (as opposed to *memento*) is an error, many of my students apparently don't believe it, because they go ahead and write *momento* anyway. I wonder about that, and sentences I get along the lines of:

> "*The* [*pengellem*] *is swinging fully against finance reform*," *Vogel said.*

It is actually quite rare for me to get an assignment with a word as badly misspelled as *pengellum,* but I'll devote a minute to this example, because I feel for the student. She was reporting on Vogel's speech, and rightly recognized that this was a good quote. There was this squirrelly *word* in it, however. She could sense it was an important word—it was what made the quote a good one, in fact—but she had no idea how to spell it. The only alternative offered by spell-check was *entellus,* which was surely wrong—and the dictionary didn't seem to be any help, either. So she just left it. This is another example of the Blind Spot Problem (BSP), the dilemma of not knowing enough to know what you don't know.

Even though I feel for her, and I recognize that the Blind Spot Problem is profound, I still wrote "NO NO NO" in the margin. What could she have done to avoid this fate?

1. Have read more. If she had, she would have come across and learned the word *pendulum.*

2. Pick up the paper dictionary and read the whole *pen-* section. There aren't that damn many words in there.

3. Alternatively, seek out friends and keep asking, "What's a word for something that swings, and starts with *pen*?" until you find someone who knows.

Back to the far more common spelling problems. Spell-check, in many ways a wonderful innovation, has caused spelling muscles— never especially robust to begin with—to atrophy to the point that they now have the firmness of mint jelly. Even worse, it's inspired a false sense of confidence, so that students would never even think of checking the spelling of a word in the dictionary.

One major consequence is a sharp increase in the number of bungled homophones—homophones being a pair of words that sound the same but mean different things. A lot of times the mistakes create unintentional humor, and make me want to concoct snarky, *New Yorker*–style headings, as in:

HE JUST WANTED TO LEND DUDES MONEY
A self described loaner, he wasn't given to hanging out and the male bonding.

IF THERE IS A MOTE AROUND YOUR HOUSE, CASE IT OUT
These zoning codes might restrict a person from building a mote around her house.

But a little of this comedy goes a long way, and in any case doesn't win your writing a great deal of respect. Here are some of the most commonly confused words; study them:

Don't confuse this . . .	with this . . .
Accept: Verb = approve of.	**Except:** Preposition or conjunction indicating difference, as in *everyone except Jon went to the party.*
Allusion: reference, usually literary.	**Elusion:** no such word. **Illusion:** fantasy. **Allude:** make reference to. **Elude:** escape. **Illude:** no such word. **Allusive:** characterized by having a lot of references. **Elusive:** hard to capture or pin down. **Illusive:** no such word. **Alusory:** no such word. **Elusory:** no such word. **Illusory:** having the qualities of an illusion.
Affect: Noun = in psychology, emotional display. (Accent on first syllable.) Verb = have an impact on.	**Effect:** Noun = impact. Verb = cause, as in *effect change.*
Aisle: corridor or row.	**Isle:** island; should be used only in proper names, such as *Isle of Man* and *British Isles.*
Bare: Adjective = naked.	**Bear:** Noun = fur-covered animal. Verb = carry, as in a burden; withstand.

Bass: (rhymes with *pass*) a kind of fish; (rhymes with *face*) a low note or the stringed instrument that plays same.	**Base:** Noun = a low common denominator; basis. Verb = establish. Adjective = low, vulgar, mean.
Capital: Noun = city that's the seat of government for a state or country; money. Adjective = uppercase, as in letter; death, as in punishment; excellent, as in idea.	**Capitol:** the building where a legislature meets; specifically, the domed building in Washington, D.C., that houses Congress.
Cite: Verb = attribute to a source. Noun (informal) = attribution.	**Sight:** Noun = eyesight. **Site:** Noun = place, frequently a Web site.
Cue: Noun = a stick you play pool with. Verb (can be followed by *up*) = prepare a record or other piece of music to be played.	**Queue (commonly British):** Noun = a line you stand in. Verb (can be followed by *up*) = wait in line.
Complimentary: free of charge; characterized by or having to do with praise, as in *a complimentary letter*.	**Complementary:** having the quality of going well together, as in *complementary colors*. (Extreme complications present themselves in the verb form. One would say, *That lipstick compliments your eyes*, even though lipstick and eyes may be *complementary* colors. Oh, well.)

Cord: string or thin rope; quantity of firewood; ribbed fabric, as in *corduroy*.	**Chord:** a pleasing combination of musical notes; (metaphorically) a feeling or emotion. One strikes a *chord*, not a *cord*.
Faze: disconcert, disturb, or distract.	**Phase:** Noun = period or stage in a process. (Interestingly, the *Star Trek* weapon is a "phaser" even though it presumably fazes its victims.)

Forward: every meaning (adjective, adverb, verb, noun) except for introductory material to a book, which is *Foreword*.

Hardy: able to withstand hardship, as in a plant.	**Hearty:** vigorous and enthusiastic, as in a laugh.
Its: possessive of *it*.	**It's:** contraction of *it is*.
Lead: Noun = the element; rhymes with *said*. Verb = first-, second-, and third-person plural present tense of *to lead*; rhymes with *heed*.	**Led:** Verb = past tense of *to lead*. (Note that past tense of *mislead* is *misled*.)
Naval: having to do with the navy.	**Navel:** the belly button and the kind of orange, because the thing at the top looks like a navel.
Palate: roof of the mouth, or, metaphorically, sense of taste.	**Palette:** tray on which a painter arranges colors, or, metaphorically, the techniques and ideas an artist draws on. **Pallet:** a small platform usually made of wood.

Past: referring to former times.	**Passed:** past tense of *pass*. On a related point, baseball is *the national pastime*, not *the national pasttime*.
Principal: Noun = the head of a school or a key participant in an enterprise. Adjective = first or among the first in importance.	**Principle:** Noun = a basic assumption or ethical standard.
There: used to indicate a place or pronoun used (with *is* or *are*) to begin a clause.	**Their:** possessive of *they*. **They're:** contraction of *they are*.
Through: preposition indicating movement from one side of something to another.	**Threw:** past tense of *throw*.
Waive: Verb = dispense with or put aside, as with a requirement or rule.	**Wave:** Noun = that in which water, air, or light travels. Verb = move around in the air.
Who's: contraction of *who is*.	**Whose:** preposition denoting ownership or association.
Your: possessive of *you*.	**You're:** contraction of *you are*.

b. The Blind Spot, Yet Again

In a particularly sloppy sort of spell-check error, the writer knows very well that he or she has typed the wrong word—or would know if he or she took even a couple of seconds to look over the sentence. The words have completely different meanings and don't sound exactly or sometimes even vaguely alike: *thought* instead of *though,* for example, *on* instead of *one,* or *weird* instead if *wired.* But the writer has come to rely on the squiggly red line, and the squiggly red line is no help. Some of these mistakes have become so common that I think the writers don't actually realize they're wrong. For example:

- *Advise* (verb) instead of *advice* (noun).

- *Breathe* (verb) instead of *breath* (noun).

- *Loose* (adjective) instead of *lose* (verb).

- Mixing up *quiet* and *quite* and *than* and *then.*

- *Where* instead of *were.*

And sometimes these substitutions can have a certain poetic rightness to them. The student who wrote, "The *eminent* [instead of *imminent*] arrival of spring marks a time for flip-flops, volleyball, and compost," and the one who said, "People will say we are America and we can not let our *hollowed* [instead of *hallowed*] education system be mocked," after the Virginia Tech shootings, made felicitous plays on words that may even have been intentional (probably not). Yet another student wrote, "In 1996, former President Bill Clinton singed the Defense of Marriage Act." No comment.

Most of the time, however, the only redeeming social value these errors have is that they're funny. You may be laughing to keep from howling with despair, but at least you're laughing. I once got an assignment with the line "You can get a descent car for $2000," which seems about right for a vehicle that can only go downhill. This nicely complemented another essay with the sentence "The narrative voice was undeniably a black man in his late thirties or early forties, educated, and possibly of middle-class decent."

And these guys can get the *New Yorker*–heading–treatment as well.

I KNEW THE CRIMINALS WERE GETTING YOUNGER, BUT THIS IS RIDICULOUS
... the 199-unit low-income housing district is a teething hotbed for drug deals and violent crime ...

CLINT ALWAYS SEEMED PRETTY NORMAL TO ME
At 74 years odd, a weathered, contemplative Eastwood portrays this inner-struggle perfectly, naturally.

I WENT TO A FIGHT AND A CITY COUNCIL MEETING BROKE OUT
The opening of the meeting was similar to past meetings with mediation and the Pledge of Allegiance.

Try it yourself, it's fun!

[PUT YOUR HEADING HERE]
Her gentile nature shines through her songs, which focus on love, growing up, and moving on.

Truth to tell, I don't always know if the people who make these mistakes are aware that they're mistakes. I do know that relying on spell-check and your instincts creates a huge blind spot as far as spelling is concerned.

c. *Eggcorns*

In 2003, linguist Geoffrey Pullum coined the term *eggcorn* to refer to common homophone or near-homophone mistakes in which the mistake makes a kind of sense. *Eggcorn* itself has a certain logic, for example, because acorns are roughly the shape of eggs. In writing and usage circles, the term caught on, and you can go to the Eggcorn Database (http://eggcorns.lascribe.net/), where, as of this writing, 631 examples are collected and defined.

Spell-check has ushered in a golden age of eggcorns, and people can be quite creative and individualistic with them. In the Introduction, I mentioned the article I once got about a board-of-education meeting that mentioned the *Super Attendant of Schools* and the one on drug problems that referred to a *heroine attic.* Others have made reference to the environmental group *the National Autobahn Society,* to *Linda B. Johnson,* to *an ex–Green Barrette,* and to the punk rocker *Sid Viscous.* I always thought he was an oily guy.

Sometimes you have to think before you realize what was meant, as in references to a newspaper's ethics policy being determined by its *On-Buzz Man* (the real word is *ombudsman*) and to the writer's fondness for going out on the town wearing a *sequence-covered dress.* Only after searching for context clues and employing the process of elimination did I realize that that a *supped up hers* was supposed to be *souped-up hearse.*

I once got an assignment that talked about a student athlete who had to miss several games because of *phenomena.* I stared at that one for a few minutes before realizing it was supposed to be, that's right, *pneumonia.* The error illustrates another spell-check problem. What probably happened is that the student took a wild stab at the spelling of the disease and then perused spell-check's suggestions. Maybe the stab was so wild that the correct spelling wasn't on the list; maybe it was and the student didn't recognize it. Who knows. The end result, in any case, was *phenomena.*

One hears a lot of these in conversation, most famously *for all ~~intensive~~ intents and purposes* and *~~Old Timer's~~ Alzheimer's disease.* Some of the others I've come upon and treasured include *It's a ~~doggy-dog~~ dog-eat-dog world* and *Any notes, quotes, or ~~antidotes~~ anecdotes?*

Some eggcorns come up so often that they now outnumber correct usages, at least in the work handed in to me. I actually expect to read that something *peaks* or *peeks* (rather than *piques*) the interest; that a person *poured* (rather than *pored*) over a book; or that a storm *wrecked* or *reeked* (as opposed to *wreaked*) havoc. Other popular ones are *hone in on* (as opposed to *home in on*); *dribble* (*drivel*); a *mute* (as opposed to *moot*) *point*; and *take the reigns* (*reins*).

Listing the eggcorns and all the other spelling mistakes is well and good, but the trouble is, if you're about to commit one, by definition, you don't know you're doing so. That's the blind spot again. The answer, again, is to cultivate an attitude of deep skepticism about your own word use. Then, if you have any smidgen of doubt about a word, DO NOT RELY ON SPELL-CHECK. Use a dictionary, preferably a paper one, and look up not only the spelling but the definition.

d. Skunked Words

I'm taking a wild guess that when some readers came to the second-to-last paragraph (the one that starts "Some eggcorns ..."), their reaction to at least one or two of the examples was "But, that's right!"

To understand why they're not, it's helpful to think about "skunked terms," a phrase coined by Bryan Garner, in his excellent book *Garner's Modern American Usage*. (No comma after *book* because Garner is the author of several outstanding tomes.) Garner explained: "When a word undergoes a marked change from one use to another—a phase that might take ten years or a hundred—it's likely to be the subject of dispute." Even as the new meaning gains popularity, traditionalists—or, as they're sometimes called, "prescriptivists"—dig in their heels and roundly condemn it as ignorant, illiterate, unacceptable, etc.

Garner observes—and I agree—"To the writer or speaker to whom credibility is important, it's a good idea to avoid distracting *any* readers," and thus he counsels avoiding these words and phrases. I agree with that, too.

The trouble is, like the language itself, the corpus of skunked words is always changing. To take just a few examples, I can remember when prescriptivists and sticklers used to grumble about the use of *contact* as a verb, as in *When are you going to contact the senator?* Hard to believe, but it's true. Obviously, they lost that battle a long time ago. Even longer ago, the expressions *champing at the bit, stamping grounds, tit-bit,* and *pom-pon* roamed the earth. Eventually (more specifically, by the end of the nineteenth century), they turned into *chomping, stomping, tidbit,* and *pom-pom.* If you used the older forms today, you would get some seriously strange looks.

Again, I'll note that writing and speaking have different standards. In conversation, getting your meaning across is really the important thing, while writing for publication or in a business, journalistic, or academic setting demands a higher standard of rules and propriety. Thus new words and new meanings gain acceptance in conversation years or even decades before they do in writing.

Going back to the list of common eggcorns, let's take a look at *duct tape,* a roll or two of which you can probably find less than fifty feet from where you're sitting. It's called *duct tape* because its original use was to tape up ducts, but *duct* is hard to say, so people started calling it "duck tape," and then people started *writing* "duck tape." You can even buy a brand of duct tape called Duck Tape. There's a fun Web site called Google Fight (http://googlefight.com) that allows you to type in a pair of words or phrases and see how many times each of them has been used on the Internet. I just staged a fight between *duck tape* and *duct tape.* *Duct tape* won, but by a relatively slim margin of 1.83 million to 1.07 million. Before too long, *duck tape* will prevail, and *duct tape* will seem as antique and dusty as *an e-mail message.* But that day is not here yet, and using *duck tape* will still make you seem a bad writer, to at least some of your readers.

A list of current skunkers is below. Once again, some may *seem* perfectly fine, but all have traditional meanings different and in some cases opposite from the ones in popular use. (If you don't believe me, look them up.) Going beyond the list, the best general way to avoid these guys is to read good writers in books and respectable publications, and follow their lead. As for an individual word, if you have any doubt as to its meaning, look it up in the dictionary. Either the skunked meaning won't be there, or it will be the fourth or fifth definition, followed by a note that says something like *nonstandard* or *objected to by some*. And Google Fight is useful as well. If a one-time skunked term wins by a standard of at least two-thirds, I hereby declare it sanitized and ready to use.

The word in the left-hand column is the current skunked term; acceptable alternative(s) follow. When the skunked term has a different meaning, it's given in parentheses.

alumni	*alumni* is correct for plural, but for singular use *alumna* (female) or *alumnus* (male).
alot	a lot
alright	all right (However, similar words such as *already* and *awhile* can can be okay if used carefully.)
bemused	amused (*Bemused* = distracted or bothered.)
cliché	(as adjective, as in *That's so cliché*); clichéd.
comprised of	composed of; made up of
couple (as in *couple things*)	couple of
disinterested	uninterested (*Disinterested* = impartial.)
fortuitous	lucky coincidence; felicitous (*Fortuitous* = accidental; unplanned.)

fun (as adjective, as in *the funnest vacation ever*)	most enjoyable, or rewrite sentence.
genius (as adjective, as in *a genius idea*)	inspired; brilliant; ingenious
grow (transitive verb, as in *grow the business*)	develop; build up
less; fewer	*Less* is used with a general, uncountable entity, as in *less water* or *less energy*, or as a general proposition: *He wanted more, but I wanted less. Fewer* is used with what can be counted: *fewer cars. Less money* means *fewer dollars.**
hopefully	I hope that
impact (as verb)	affect; have an impact on
myself (as subject, as in *Jesse and myself spent the whole day in the library*)	I
nonplussed	unfazed; nonchalant (*Nonplussed* = taken aback.)

---

* I haven't been able to find a source to back me up on this, but I have always maintained that *less* should be used when the quantity is one, as in the song lyric "One less bell to answer." I also insist that supermarket signs reading "Five items or less" are correct, since the phrase *than that* is understood at the end.

novel	book (*Novel* = book-length work of fiction, as opposed to drama, poetry, or nonfiction.)
notorious, infamous	famous (*Notorious, infamous* = famous for something bad.)
penultimate	ultimate (*Penultimate* = second to last.)
phenomena (as singular)	phenomenon
presently	currently; now (*Presently* = shortly; soon.)
verbal	oral; spoken (*Verbal* = in or having to do with words.)

One short skunked word and its relatives demand a fuller explanation. The word is *they* when used as an "epicene pronoun" (EP), that is, in place of a singular antecedent. For example:

1. [*Any student who wants to attend the game should bring their ID card to the ticket window.*]

2. [*Arcade Fire and about 20,000 of their fans turned the PNC Center into a raucous party Thursday night.*]

3. [*The Court Street Pub is changing to their summer menu this week.*]

The EP has a lot of arguments in its favor. In example 1, replacing *their* with *his* would sound sexist; *her* sounds like you're trying too hard *not* to be sexist; and *his or her* could come off as stilted. Meanwhile, using *it* for a rock band just sounds weird. Consequently, the EP—and all three of the above examples—are perfectly fine in conversation. I predict that they'll be acceptable in formal writing in ten years, fifteen at the maximum. However, they're not acceptable now, so you have to make adjustments.

> *1. Any student who wants to attend the game should bring his or her ID card to the ticket window.*

A write-around is even better:

> *If you want to attend the game, you have to bring your ID card to the ticket window.*

> *2. Arcade Fire and about 20,000 fans turned the PNC Center into a raucous party Thursday night.*

> *3. The Court Street Pub is changing to its summer menu this week.*

(For Skunked Grammar, see II.C.2.d.)

3. WRONG WORD

The spell-check errors and the eggcorns get the headlines and the laughs, but a more common and insidious problem is word choices that are off, sometimes by just a hair, sometimes by a Howard Stern wig and a full beard. Too often, reading student papers is like listening to a routine by Norm Crosby, the malapropeptic comedian who referred to having a good "rappaport" with a like-minded friend. Here are some real-life examples, with what I guess to be the right word in parenthesis:

> On the Mason-Dixon Line: An Anthology of Contemporary Delaware Writers ~~exemplifies~~ *(consists of—but even better would be* is) *a collection of essays, poems, and short stories by Delaware's own authors.*

> *Of the many things the students ~~aspired~~ (expected) to see, a terrorist attack was not one of them.*

> *. . . the drop in candidates can be ~~accredited~~ (attributed) to . . .*

> *Stories about the hurricane ~~invade~~ (dominate) the entire first section of the newspaper.*

> *No one can ~~blame~~ (accuse) John Henrickson of being an apathetic college student.*

> *The vast ~~proportion~~ (majority) of students is enrolled in the College of Arts and Science.*

> *She said it was her father's participation in the army which ~~possessed~~ (inspired, motivated) her to join the College Republicans.*

Then there's this one, which seems to encapsulate all the problems students are having:

> *The land, which is currently occupied ~~with~~ (by) older, run-down homes, will be rejuvenated* (I'm not sure what the right word is—I just know that rejuvenated isn't it) *to fit the positive ~~stigma~~ (image) that the city ~~manager~~ (is trying) to uphold.*

How to fix or avoid the problem? Again, it's a toughie. There's not much more you can do than undertake a close scrutiny of your writing, dictionary in hand. Be very wary of the online thesaurus. If you are having problems with word choice, you also might do well to find a smart, well-read friend and agree to read each other's work.

One common wrong-word subcategory happens when writers have a decent idea in mind and start it off well, but aren't rigorous about matching up their subjects and verbs. Consider:

> [*Investigations at that time did not uncover the source of the outbreak, and the number of infections soon ceased.*]

Well, infections may have ceased, but *numbers* don't cease. The fix is simple:

> *Investigations at that time did not uncover the source of the outbreak, and infections soon ceased.*

Similarly, in

> [*In the past two years the national unemployment rate has doubled and is at a high that falls second to only one other peak in history, occurring in the 1980s.*]

the word *fall* doesn't really belong and got the writer in trouble. Various adjustments could be made to spruce the sentence up, but at the very least you can say:

> *In the past two years, the national unemployment rate has doubled; it's now at a high that is second to only one other peak in history, occurring in the 1980s.*

D. Grammar

As I suggested in the introduction, grammatical mistakes are overrated—by which I mean they get a disproportionate amount of attention as a source of bad writing. By definition, native speakers of a language know its grammar. No American above the age of four would say, "Him gave the book to I." However, we might say, "Peter and him went to the movie with Sarah and I," which is nonstandard, or, to put it bluntly, wrong.

That, like virtually every other common grammatical "mistake," is an instance of vernacular or colloquial expressions clashing with the standards of formal or public writing and usage. The mistakes fall into three categories: *Sanitized, Skunked,* and *Still Wrong.*

1. SANITIZED

This refers to usages that at one time were verboten but, over the decades and sometimes centuries, have become acceptable to everybody, or just about everybody. In fact, in most of these cases, the formerly "correct" usage now sounds either too formal or just plain weird. However, you may have a supervisor, editor, or teacher who sticks to the old-fashioned dicta. If so, he or she, unfortunately, is the boss and nothing I say or write can change that. Still, you have my permission to wave this section in the air and protest that you read in a book that it's perfectly acceptable to:

a. End a Sentence with a Preposition

Who are you going to the movies with? (But see III.C.7.)

b. Use *Who* Instead of *Whom* in the Objective Case

Who are you going to the movies with?

The exception is immediately following a preposition: *To whom should I send the customer-satisfaction survey?*

c. Use Objective Rather than Subjective Pronouns in Comparisons, Following the Verb *to Be*, and in First-Person Plural

They have a bigger house than us. (Alternatively: *than we do.*)

Hello, it's me.

We are all at the mercy of Mother Nature. But especially us astronomers.

d. Judiciously Split Infinitives

To avoid damaging the wall, you ~~carefully~~ have to carefully hold the picture hook and hammer it in.

e. (And Similarly) Break up a Compound Verb with an Adverb

He has frequently woken up ~~frequently~~ in the morning with no idea where he spent the night.

f. Use *Like* (I)

This little word, depending on the way it's used, can be alternately sanitized, skunked, and still wrong. (And that's not even getting into the way young people famously use it in conversation, as a filler ["I'm, like, tired"] or indicator of attribution ["He was like, 'Why aren't you going to the concert?'"]. Even young people know enough not to use it this way in formal writing.)

It wasn't necessarily always the case, but it's now okay to use *like:* As a synonym for *such as.*

We read authors like Hemingway, Faulkner, and Fitzgerald.

To introduce a clause where a verb is omitted.

He takes to engineering like a duck [takes] to water.

He speaks French like a native [does].

It has never been wrong or even suspect to use *like* in a sentence like:

Like Paris, Rome has an almost unlimited number of world-class restaurants.

However, some people are gun-shy about *like* and engage in the hoity toity lingo that's called "hypercorrection."

[*In common with Paris, Rome has an almost unlimited number of world-class restaurants.*]

Actually, *in common with* is called for in only one situation: sentences like *Bill and Paul have lot in common.*

g. Use a Plural Verb with a Collective Noun

A number of objections ~~comes~~ come to mind.

In the above sentence, the plural *come* is better than the singular *comes,* even though (singular) *number* is ostensibly the subject of the sentence. That's because the emphasis is on *objections.* By the same logic, if the emphasis is on the singular collective, the singular verb is preferable:

> *Just one battalion of soldiers* ~~*were*~~ *was sent to the front.*

> *A bucket of worms* ~~*were*~~ *was on top of the bench.*

> *He was one of the employees who* ~~*was*~~ *were given an award at the ceremony.*

Often, it could go either way, as in this pair:

1. *A scrum of applicants was hovering outside the office door by 7* a.m.

2. *A scrum of applicants were hovering outside the office door by 7* a.m.

Which do you prefer? I would go with 2.

2. SKUNKED

As with words, certain grammatical constructions are considered okay by some or most authorities but retain an offensive odor for many readers (and, crucially, teachers and editors), and should be avoided. This shouldn't present a problem, since they're usually not difficult to replace with the correct form.

a. First-Person First

[*I and Matt will be collecting tickets for the concert.*]

Matt and I will be collecting tickets for the concert.

b. Like (II)

Some have argued that the 1950s ad slogan "Winston tastes good like a cigarette should" started the modern prescriptivist movement. In any case, things have gotten to the point where using *like* instead of *as, as if,* or *as though* is widely accepted. But it still could get you in hot water in certain quarters.

[*He looked like he really wanted to jump into the pool.*]

He looked as though he really wanted to jump into the pool.

[*Like the professor said, this material will be covered on the exam.*]

As the professor said, this material will be covered on the exam.

c. Possessive Before a Gerund

This one is on the cusp and may get a clean bill of health before the decade is out. But for now it's a skunker.

[*I don't like you talking about the senator in that tone.*]

I don't like your talking about the senator in that tone.

d. Past Tense

The word *snuck* did not appear in print before 1887, at least according to *The Oxford English Dictionary*. Traditionally, the past tense of *to sneak* had always been *sneaked.* Then *snuck* sneaked in, presumably because *sneaked* is hard to speak. By now, *The Random House Dictionary* deems it "a standard variant past tense and past participle" of *sneak*. In Google Fight, *snuck* beats *sneaked* by a nearly two-to-one margin.

That means, for all intents and purposes, that it's okay. The same goes for *hung* and *dove,* which have respectively joined *hanged* and *dived* as accepted. Not so with these other relatively recent verb forms, in which the traditional participle is more and more commonly used as the past tense. They are all still skunked.

He ~~drunk~~ *drank* the water.

The fish ~~layed laid~~ *lay* on the counter, filleted and ready to broil.

(That is past tense of the verb *lie,* which is often confused with the verb *lay. Lie* is intransitive—you, or fish, do it all by yourself. *Lay* is transitive, meaning that you do it to something, like carpet or your burdens; it's often followed by *down.* ~~I lay~~ laid *the files on my desk.*)

Honey, I ~~shrunk~~ shrank the kids.

In a fit of pique, he ~~sunk~~ sank the toy boat.

The Basie Band really ~~swung~~ swang.

e. *Ly*-Less Adverbs

A common move in spoken English is streamlining adverbs.

[*This was a real nice clambake.*]

[*Think different.*]

[*He didn't do so bad.*]

[*That car sure drives smooth.*]

I bracketed those sentences with a heavy heart because they have such a nice, casual sound to them. Hey: I even called this book *How to Not Write Bad*! Unfortunately, this sort of thing is still skunked in writing meant for anything more formal than a blog post. The first, second, and third examples are easily changed:

This was a really nice clambake. (Apologies to Oscar Hammerstein.)

Think differently. (Apologies to Steve Jobs.)

He didn't do so badly.

However, the third runs into a problem that's illuminated by a famous bit of dialogue from the movie *Airplane:*

RUMACK: *Can you fly this plane, and land it?*
STRIKER: *Surely you can't be serious.*
RUMACK: *I am serious . . . and don't call me Shirley.*

Surely is a hard word to pull off. Moreover, as in the bracketed example, the adverbial *sure* is sometimes used to mean something slightly different from *surely*. Here, the best tack might be seeking out another word altogether.

That car certainly [or definitely, or really] drives smoothly.

There are some exceptions. When a verb indicates a state of being—that is, if it could theoretically be replaced by the verb *to be*—it should be followed by the non *-ly*, or adjective, form.
You look beautiful. I feel good. I feel great. I feel bad. I feel fine. I feel pretty. The dinner tasted wonderful.
[*I feel badly*] and [*the dinner tasted wonderfully*] are hypercorrection.

An apparent exception to *this* is the word *well,* especially in negative sentences. (It's only an apparent exception because in this context, *well* is an adjective, as in *well-baby clinic.*) So we say, *He didn't feel well, so he stayed home from work.*

f. Only, the Lonely

For a little word, *only* creates a heap of difficulties. For a century or more, it was a sticklers' article of faith that this adverb had to be placed directly in front of the word it was modifying, or else all sorts of ambiguous hell would break loose. Thus, the sticklers would have had you write:

> *I have eyes only for you.*

> *Only God knows what I'd be without you.*

> *I want to be with only you.*

Music fans of a certain advanced age will recognize these as mangled and ruined versions of the titles of some classic pop songs: "I Only Have Eyes for You," "God Only Knows (What I'd Be Without You)," and "I Only Want to Be with You."

Here's the thing. In pop songs and in speech, please feel free to put *only* in any position that feels right and seems to make sense. In formal or public writing, however, the sticklers' rule about placement still applies. (Barely.)

> *He ~~only~~ has only one more course to take before graduation.*

Germany's economy ~~only~~ grew by only 1 percent last year.

I'm ~~only~~ asking only for a little respect.

g. Assorted Grammatically Skunked Expressions

[*He couldn't help but be impressed.*]

He couldn't help being impressed.

———————

[*It's not that big of a deal.*]

It's not that big a deal.

———————

[*I'm a person that likes to laugh.*]

I'm a person who likes to laugh.

3. STILL WRONG

Certain grammatical mistakes are commonly made in spoken but not written English, and thus won't be addressed at length in this book. Examples include *ain't; of* instead of *have* in expressions like *He could of come; them* instead of *those* in expressions like *one of them things;* and regionalisms like *He done wrecked the car.* The one that probably comes up the most—as it's a feature of many nonstandard dialects, including African-American Vernacular

English—is a transposition of past and participle forms of irregular verbs.

[*He seen it coming.*]

He saw it coming.

———————

[*I had went to watch that movie when it first come out.*]

I had gone to watch that movie when it first came out.

a. Subjunctive

The subjunctive mood has been losing sway in the English language over the centuries, but it's still got some sway left. Basically, the subjunctive calls for a shift in the verb *to be* in reference to untrue scenarios; the word *if* is usually a giveaway.

[*If I was you, I would take that class.*]

If I were you, I would take that class.

Note that if the scenario followed by *if* is not necessarily untrue—that is, if it's in doubt—the standard past tense is called for, and the subjunctive is hypercorrection.

[*I asked him if he were happy with our marriage.*]

I asked him if he was happy with our marriage.

[*Check what's in the refrigerator to find out if he were in the house last night.*]

Check what's in the refrigerator to find out if he was in the house last night.

b. Like (III)

Like still doesn't cut the mustard when it's followed by *in*:

[*Like in France, American TV is a case of dumb and dumber.*]

As in France, American TV is a case of dumb and dumber.

That's an easy fix, but a comparable misuse of *unlike* is more challenging.

[*Unlike in the higher atmospheres, airplanes frequently encounter turbulence when they're about to land.*]

Airplanes often run into turbulence when they're about to land. That's not true in higher atmospheres.

c. (Don't) Let 'Em Dangle

A similar *like* mistake is:

[*Like his first trial, Morgan was acquitted.*]

Again, the fix is to use *as in:*

As in his first trial, Morgan was acquitted.

This error is an example of a dangling modifier. Here are some more examples from students' writing:

[*By including several charts along with the story, readers are encouraged to understand the long-term trends.*]

[*Being the most spectacular event of the year, newspapers were obligated to devote major coverage to the hurricane.*]

[*As an expert on fiscal recovery, his comments were listened to with intense interest.*]

[*By reversing the color scheme, the eye is captured.*]

[*Claiming to be a simple man leading an ordinary life of a male as he enjoys watching football with his buddy's, Smith's lifestyle is far from ordinary*]. (For *buddy's,* see "Apostrophes," II.B.1.)

(From a review of a new bra by Victoria's Secret) [*Sitting in class or dancing at the bar, the bra performed well . . . Though slightly pricey, your breasts will thank you.*]

The grammatical problem in those sentences (and I apologize if I seem to be stating the obvious) is that *Morgan* didn't resemble his first trial; *readers* didn't include the charts; *newspapers* were not the most spectacular event; the eye doesn't reverse the color scheme; *his comments* were not an expert; *Smith's lifestyle* didn't claim to be a simple man; *the bra* doesn't sit in class or dance at a bar; and the reader's *breasts* are not pricey. (Pause for snarky comment.) In each case, the italicized word or phrase is the subject of the sentence, and the opening phrase—up to the comma, that is—has to modify, describe, or characterize the subject and nothing but the subject.

To get technical for just a minute, I'll note that this is a problem only with introductory *phrases* (which do not contain a subject and verb), not *clauses* (which do). So there is no dangler issue in the following:

> *Since he is running for mayor next year, he is resigning all his board memberships.* (Opens with dependent clause.)

> *Kris is the starting center on the basketball team, but Jessica wants to replace her.* (Opens with independent clause.)

An interesting thing about danglers is that a rather select group of writers commit them: the minority who would even *attempt* a complex sentence. They haven't quite mastered the skill of putting one of these together, and thus can get themselves in rather spectacular trouble, but at least they realize that this level of complexity is, as Hamlet said, a consummation devoutly to be wished.

Relevant as well is that danglers are very common—and, to a certain extent, acceptable—in speech. When talking, some "mistakes" are okay. Did you notice that the previous sentence has a dangling modifier (mistakes don't talk)? In conversation, I bet you wouldn't. As another example, let's suppose I'm speaking with someone who's an expert in ancient religion, and I say: "As an expert in ancient religion, I wonder what you think of devil worship." That is a dangling modifier: "I" am not a religion expert. In speech, we give this a pass. In writing, we—and by *we* I mean the professors and editors of the world—do not.

That's unfortunate, because danglers spring incessantly from many writers' fingers; it takes a substantial amount of discipline and rigor to prune them from our prose. (If you haven't guessed, I am one of those writers.) Consequently, much more so than the other errors on my list, they show up in well-respected publications, such as the *New York Times Book Review* (*rather than providing the meticulous examination of the process of looking . . . we are treated to rhetorical flights that provide little perspective of any useful kind*), the *New Yorker* (*A major political donor, his greatest concern is to protect Israel*), and the *Chronicle of Higher Education* (*Having made it successfully through all three gantlets, all of the rejections I experienced along the way have become only vague memories*).

How to avoid danglers? A simple strategy will help you smoke these bad boys out. First of all, you have to recognize sentences that have this structure: MODIFIER-COMMA-SUBJECT-VERB. The vast majority of the time, the part of such a sentence before the comma will either:

- Begin with *Like, Unlike,* or *As.* (Example: *Like most of the student body, Rogoff has spent an inordinate amount of time avoiding hard classes.*)

- Contain a gerund, that is, a verb in the *—ing* form. (*Being an inquisitive sort, I wonder what you ate for breakfast.*)

- Begin with the infinitive form of a verb. (*To maximize your chances of losing weight, you should avoid fried food.*)

- Begin with one or more participles. (*Shaken and not stirred, James Bond's martinis are a twentieth-century icon.*)

- Consist of a noun phrase. (*A popular mayor, Potter is running unopposed for reelection.*)

Once you recognize the sentence, circle the subject, the modifier, and the verb. Then see if it makes sense if you keep all the elements but change the order to this: SUBJECT-COMMA-MODIFIER-COMMA-VERB. If it does—as in all of the examples above—you're good to go. If it doesn't, you have a dangler.

So take one of my students' troubled sentences:

[*Being the most spectacular event of the year, newspapers devoted major coverage to the hurricane.*]

Shifted, it would be:

[*Newspapers, being the most spectacular event of the year, devoted major coverage to the hurricane.*]

Obviously no good. There are any number of ways to fix this sentence. Probably the best thing to do is to follow the student's original instinct and start with the hurricanes. So:

The hurricane was the most spectacular event of the year,
and newspapers devoted major coverage to it.

To make matters even more complicated, danglers are some-times okay.

That sentence is an example of a certain class of opening modi-fiers, sometimes referred to as *sentence adverbs*, that get a pass when it comes to the whole dangling-modifier question. These are words or phrases that, rather than modify the subject, convey the speaker's or writer's attitude, or generally characterize the content of the rest of the sentence. For example:

Fortunately, the game will go on as scheduled.

To be perfectly honest, that course is pure hogwash.

Summing up this section, it's pretty easy to spot a dangling modifier.

d. Parallel Universes

The parallelism problem crops up most commonly in lists. You want to make sure that every item is in the same basic form.

[I like to hike, play disk golf, and just goofing off.]

In the example above, the phrase *I like to* applies to the first two items in the list, but is mysteriously dropped for the third. As the Beatles once sang, "You can't do that." So change to:

I like hiking, playing disk golf, and just goofing off.

Sometimes, you need to just be listless:

[*He has experience in copyediting, graphics, and has won two professional awards.*]

He has experience in copyediting and graphics, and has won two professional awards.

The alluring phrase *as well as* creates a parallel problem in 1, below. It's technically fixed in 2, but the sentence is awkward (a word you will run into again in Part III, many times).

1. [*World AIDS Day is devoted to spreading further awareness of HIV and AIDS, as well as a time of remembrance for the millions who have died because of the virus.*]

2. [*World AIDS Day is devoted to spreading further awareness of HIV and AIDS and is a time of remembrance for the millions who have died because of the virus.*]

3. *World AIDS Day is devoted to spreading further awareness of HIV and AIDS. It's a time of remembrance for the millions who have died because of the virus.*

e. The Sports Conditional

This isn't exclusively found in a sports context, but for some reason, athletes, fans, and commentators are unaccountably drawn to the phrase *would have* in considering scenarios that didn't happen.

[*If Johnson would have caught that ball, the Bisons would have won the game.*]

If Johnson had caught the ball, the Bisons would have won the game.

The sports conditional seems particularly irresistible when wishing or hoping is involved:

"I wish I would have took a swing at that ball," Prendergast said.

Well, you can't change a quotation, but if Prendergast were *writing* his sentiments, the correct grammar would be:

I wish I had taken a swing at that ball.

Not technically an error, but pretty hackneyed, is "the sports present," in which athletes and sportswriters recite hypothetic or conditional events in the present tense.

[*If he makes that interception, the whole game changes.*]

If he had made that interception, the whole game would have changed.

f. Between You and I, This One Bears Some Study

Take a look at this sentence and try to spot the problem word:

> [*It would be great if you could come to the concert with my wife and I.*]

It's the shortest and final one, *I.* Traditional grammar dictates that it should be replaced with *me,* on the principle that prepositions (such as *with*) are followed by the objective (*me*) rather than the subjective case (*I*).

> *It would be great if you could come to the concert with my wife and me.*

When only one pronoun is involved, absolutely no one has trouble with the principle. No one, that is, would write:

> [*It would be great if you could come to the concert with I.*]

Yet many, many people have problems when there are two or more elements in the noun phrase, especially when one of the elements is a pronoun indicating the speaker or writer.

> [*Between you and I, that project is a disaster.*]

> [*The teacher gave the assignment to she and I.*]

Between you and me, that project is a disaster.

The teacher gave the assignment to her and me.

Some authorities, notably Steven Pinker of Harvard, have argued in favor of the subjective case in this situation, thus provoking the wrath of traditionalists. The argument is that (drawing from the above examples) *my wife and I, you and I,* and *she and I* are better viewed as self-contained units than as a combination of pronouns. And, as units, they can be either object or subject. It's the same (Pinker would contend) as a title like *The King and I.* And no one would write, *I won two tickets to see* The King and Me.

I have to admit I see the logic in the argument. But it doesn't matter. Long and at this point unbreakable custom dictates that you must write *my wife and me, you and me,* and *her and me* in these cases.

g. Whomever

This word has only slightly higher grammatical standing than *ain't,* but it's used by millions more people. It yields 11.7 million hits on Google and more than 1,000 on Google News, which consists of articles written in the last month or so by professional and semiprofessional writers. The most recent (posted just two hours ago as I write) came from the Web site of New York City's Fox News affiliate:

> [*Meat Loaf has a bone to pick with whomever started the rumor that he passed out at a balloon festival in New Jersey this past weekend.*]

Like an overwhelming majority of the examples on Google News (and in my students' work), *whomever* is incorrect here. You can see why the writer made the mistake—*with* is a preposition, and prepositions are traditionally followed by the objective case. But *whomever started the rumor, etc.* is a unit—a noun phrase, to be exact—so the correct word to kick it off is *whoever.*

Whomever has gotten so popular that people have started to use it even when there's not a preposition to be found in the immediate area. A subject heading on a gamers' bulletin board reads: "ATTN: Whomever owns zombieland server." No excuse for that.

As you proceed on life's journey, you may be tempted to use *whomever.* Resist the temptation, except in two relatively rare cases.

1. It's the last word in the sentence and is immediately followed by a verb other than *to be* or by a preposition. *I'll go with whomever.*

2. It's a true object. *The doctors will treat whomever the sick boy coughed on.*

Looking at the awkwardness of those two sentences, I'm going to amend my rule, as follows:

Never use *whomever.*

h. Fragments of My Imagination

Sentence fragments (SFs) are a weird mistake. For one thing, virtually every professional writer uses them. Including me. *Including me,* of course, is a SF. It's defined as a collection of words that's *treated* as a sentence (that is, the first letter is capitalized and a period, question mark, or exclamation point comes at the end) but, because it doesn't contain both subject and verb, doesn't have the grammatical standing of a sentence.

Despite their popularity and usefulness, SFs earn some serious wrath in virtually every writing handbook on my shelf. The trouble is the examples these books give. Almost none of them are recognizable as anything that comes across my desk or appears on my computer screen. For example, *The Little, Brown Handbook* gives this as an instance of what not to do:

> *With the links, users can move to other Web sites. That they want to consult.*

In twenty years of teaching, I've never had something like that handed in to me. There are a dozen or more examples in the chapter, and the only one that rings slightly true is this:

> *Uncle Marlon drew out his tales. And embellished them.*

The thing is, I don't particularly mind the Uncle Marlon SF. Which leads me to a possibly useful generalization. (I hope you noticed that the previous sentence was a SF.) Sentence fragments can be acceptable and effective, in all but the most formal writing, if they come following a deliberate pause for effect. And if they're used sparingly! (I can't stop.) Reading aloud is especially important here. If you do, you'll find that sometimes the pause is for humor (that talkative Marlon), sometimes for drama, sometimes for irony, and sometimes merely for emphasis.

So.

All that being said, an ill-conceived SF can be a really bad mistake. I do occasionally get them handed in to me. For example:

> [*Of the students surveyed only 138 knew it was advised by the CDC to be tested for HIV annually when engaged in risky behavior. Classified as having multiple partners, unprotected relations, or regular work in risky medical fields*].

> *Of the students surveyed, only 138 knew the CDC advises annual HIV tests for people who engage in "risky behavior," defined as having multiple partners or unprotected sexual relations, or working in risky medical fields.*

If an SF is pointed out on a piece of your writing by a teacher, supervisor, or writer, I would advise you to eschew fragments for six months, during which time you'll likely come to a better understanding of what a sentence is and isn't. At that point, you can start playing around with SFs again. End of advice. And end of Part II.

PART III

How to Not Write Bad

If you've absorbed the previous chapter, you've achieved—or are well on your way to achieving—the goal of removing the mistakes and errors from your writing. The next step is getting rid of a collection of qualities that aren't technically wrong but are eminently undesirable. The best way to sum them up is with a simple chart:

Bad	Not Bad
Wordy or pretentious	Concise, straightforward
Vague	Precise
Awkward	Graceful, fluid
Ambiguous or misleading	Clear
Clichéd, hackneyed, or pat	Fresh

That's pretty much it. Of course, there are a lot of additional elements associated with writing *well*, or *very well*: brilliant similes and metaphors, masterful deploying of irony and other registers, humor, a personal voice, an ear for and ability to mimic *other* writers' and speakers' voices, a command of pacing and structure, the ability to construct long and complex sentences in the manner of Samuel Johnson, a sure and creative hand with metaphor and other figures of speech, a capacious vocabulary and the ability to use it, a sense of audience, an appreciation for subtlety, and so on.

But those are topics for another book. Writing not-bad is quite enough for this one. Before getting to the particulars, I'll review the general approach to take. First, turn off the radio, the iPod, the television; put your phone on silence and in your pocket; X out of or minimize all screens other than the one you're writing on. Multitasking = bad writing.

Second, know what you want to say. Any sort of uncertainty, fuzziness, or equivocation in your thoughts multiplies on the page and yields very bad writing. The boys in *Entourage* are always telling each other to "Hug it out"; my mantra for you is "Think it out." You will often realize that you have to find out some more about your subject before you set words to paper. This is called research. Do it.

Third, be a mindful writer. A good homemaker doesn't just fling silverware and plates on the table, but arranges them consciously and carefully. A stylish dresser chooses an outfit carefully. Be that kind of writer. Read each sentence aloud—literally, at first. Eventually you will develop an inner ear that will allow you to note the awkwardness, wordiness, word repetition, and vagueness that are the hallmarks of mindless, bad writing. And eventually, you will streamline the process and "hear" yourself write. And that is pretty cool.

A. Punctuation

1. QUOTATION MARKS

As a rule, stay away from using quotation marks except to indicate a title (*"Gone with the Wind" was Clark Gable's greatest role*) or a quotation (*"Take me home," she said*). Avoid, that is, the use of air quotes and scare quotes.

> [*I have always considered him a "brother from another mother."*]

> [*My roommate thinks Lady Gaga is "the bomb."*]

> [*After a while, things got "hot and heavy."*]

That is bad writing. My sense is that the quotes are the punctuational equivalent of a phrase like "just kidding" or "I'm just sayin'"—that is, a way to absolve yourself after using a cliché. People: a cliché is a cliché, whether or not it's in quotes. There is no absolution. (See III.B.4.) Some of the time, you're going to have to do the work of finding a fresh way to say what you mean.

> *Ever since we showed up on the first day of first grade wearing the same* Star Wars *T-shirt, there's been this odd mystical bond between us.*

However, if you really believe in the phrase, have the courage of your convictions (not "courage of your convictions") and use it naked:

My roommate thinks Lady Gaga is the bomb.

After a while, things got hot and heavy.

2. EXCLAMATION POINTS, DASHES, SEMICOLONS, COLONS, PARENTHESES, ITALICS, AND RHETORICAL QUESTIONS . . .

. . . can all be effective if used correctly and in moderation. Common mistakes and misuses are addressed in Part II. The overuse issue is worth taking a couple of minutes with. When I was a magazine editor a few decades ago, I noticed that when some of the writers I worked with underlined or italicized a word for emphasis, sure as shooting, another underlined word or phrase would pop up within a couple of lines. And then another. I have continued to note this in published work, and have come to think of it as comparable to a phenomenon that occurs in concert halls: just as the sound of one person coughing makes other audience members powerless to resist the urge, so one use of italics can be contagious.

Sometimes the issue is less power of suggestion and more personal predilection. Tom Wolfe is enamored of exclamation points, John Irving of semicolons (examine his books and you'll see what I mean), the *New Yorker* magazine of commas, and Ben Yagoda of parentheses. Emily Dickinson was quite fond of dashes. I don't know about those other worthies, but quite a lot of my revising time is spent getting rid of parens (while still keeping enough of them for my writing to *sound* like me). If you've got a go-to typographical move, this is the strategy to follow.

A couple of pieces of punctuation are worth special mention. The first is exclamation points! Or, rather, the first is exclamation points. They've spread way beyond Tom Wolfe: if you've spent any time on e-mail, Facebook, or Twitter these days, you know that they are the punctuational coin of the realm. Sometimes, one isn't enough, and you need two, three, or even four to show adequate enthusiasm. In fact, when I first got into texting with my twenty-two-year-old daughter, Maria, I was ending sentences with periods, as is my wont. She told me to use either exclamation points or nothing: the periods made it seem that I was being ironic or pointedly unenthusiastic. But what's good for texting is bad for text. That is, stay away from exclamation points, except, as a matter of fact, when you're being ironic or playful. Like this! Even then, use them sparingly.*

And what of the rhetorical question? It's definitely overused, often serving as nothing more than artificial throat clearing at the beginning of a paragraph. Instead, it usually works better to just dive right into what you want to say. The RQ can be a useful device, but it has to be deployed skillfully. As my first boss, Myron "Mike" Kolatch, the longtime editor of the *New Leader* magazine, used to say: "When you ask a question, answer it immediately"—the way I

---

* As I've noted, I teach journalism, and beginning reporters are often tempted to overuse exclamation points in quoted material: "'I hope we have a great year!' the coach said." That doesn't come off well. If you use exclamation points at all in quotes, save them for when the speaker is screaming his or her lungs out.

did at the beginning of this paragraph. That's as opposed to something like:

> [*Is City Hall in compliance with new federal energy regulations? In 2007, Congress passed legislation requiring…*]

No good: that question just lies there, unanswered, puzzling or bewildering the reader. First tell us about the regulations, then address the issue of whether or not City Hall is following them.

B. Words and Phrases

1. REALLY QUICK FIX: AVOID THESE WORDS!

Some writing adjustments are hard. But eliminating or at least sharply reducing these words from your prose is painless and shows swift results.

a. *Unique*

Unique is a much-hated word, but I actually hate it for different reasons than most people do. The most frequent complaint is that it technically means *one of a kind* but is commonly used to mean *unusual*:

> [*The most unique thing about him is that he has a fauxhawk.*]

The argument goes that there are no degrees of uniqueness; either a thing is unique or it isn't. Consequently:

> *He has a fauxhawk.*

Or take a look at these two sentences from a student's profile of a librarian (whose name has been changed):

> [*When the thought of a typical librarian comes to mind, Associate Librarian Raymond McCarthy tries to steer clear of the typical stereotypes associated with the other employees working in the campus library. His everyday attire and approachability prove that he is much more unique than the average librarian.*]

Unique is hardly the only problem in the passage; wordiness, stereotyping, cliché, and a dangling modifier come to mind right off the bat. But the U-word, along with the repetition of *typical*, is probably the most easily addressed. That is, if you want to say he's approachable and wears everyday attire, just say so, and leave the issue of uniqueness out of it. (Of course, it would be better to specify exactly what he's wearing, and give an example of his approachability.)

Nonunique *unique* is certainly something to be concerned with, but even worse, to me, is the now very common use of *unique* as a synonym for *admirable, impressive,* or some quality that is vaguely positive but has no other attributes. For an assignment in which students were asked to nominate a Web site for the Pulitzer Prize in online journalism, someone in my class wrote:

> [*The criteria that made this site able to be nominated are because of the uniqueness of the content it possesses.*]

Again, one looks on a veritable cavalcade of infelicities, leading off with bad parallelism, infelicitous use of the passive, and wordiness. What's being said, I think, is:

> *The site has excellent content.*

Then there's this:

> [*Iron Hill is a unique restaurant that's a favorite for Homecoming and Graduation.*]

Not only is that advertising-speak, but it's *bad* advertising-speak. If you take the effort to find out or figure out something real (the opposite of advertising-speak), you will produce a stronger sentence.

> *Iron Hill is already fully booked for Homecoming and Graduation.*

I'll pause here because the above example illustrated a point that's going to come up again and again in this section. Being *unique*-less isn't the only reason why the second version is better. It also has a piece of relevant and specific information: the fact that the restaurant is sold out. The writer of the first sentence doesn't know much about Iron Hill—other than a vague sense that it's popular—and has produced weak writing. The writer of the second sentence has taken the trouble to find out an important fact and has used it to produce strong writing.

This is no coincidence. If you are un- or underinformed about your subject, you will hem and haw, engage in the passive voice and qualifiers, and overgeneralize. If you take the trouble to fully research it—and, equally important, think hard and rigorously about it—you'll be specific, precise, and authoritative. In other words, knowledge leads to good writing. That is simply a corollary of perhaps the most important of all writing mantras: *show, don't tell.*

This issue never, ever goes away, because telling is much easier than showing. You can sit back in your easy chair, pluck a few adjectives out of the thesaurus, and you're off to the races. To show, you have to get up off your butt: literally, by doing some research and reporting, or figuratively, by going beyond your initial top-of-the-head thought and lifting and arranging some nouns and verbs.

(I hereby give you permission to use *unique* if you really and truly mean that the thing being described is one of a kind, cross your heart.)

b. *Literally*

In conversation, it's no big deal to use *literally* when you mean *figuratively.* If you said, for example, "I literally turned the house upside down looking for that checkbook," your listeners would understand that your house is still on its foundation. However, this *literally* literally makes for bad habits and therefore bad writing. No one will misunderstand you, but your readers will raise a collective eyebrow. You might be tempted to use the word when it's technically correct—for example, writing *I was literally up all night* in reference to a night in which you did not sleep. Resist the temptation and stay away from *literally*. It's stronger and cleaner to serve the facts straight up: *I was up all night.*

c. *Myself*

The English language is being inundated with *myself*s, the result, I think, of creeping wordiness and uncertainty in many cases over whether *I* or *me* is correct. So we get a lot of:

> [*The people signing the document were George Parkinson, Leila Fischer, and myself.*]

> [*The other players and myself left the field soon afterward.*]

In the second example, *myself* should be replaced with *I.* That's true in the first example as well, but it's not as obvious. You can avoid the uncertainty—and improve the sentence—by recasting it:

> *George Parkinson, Leila Fischer, and I signed the document.*

The bottom line is to use *myself* only when you (the speaker or writer) are the object of the verb (*I looked at myself in the mirror and have to admit I was smokin'*) or as a way to emphasize that you were the sole actor (*I put up the bookcases myself*). Otherwise, dispense with it.

d. Share

Share is fine to signify "generously distribute," as in *He shared his cookies with the other students.* But it is not fine as a psychobabbly replacement for *say* or *discuss*, as in *He shared that he plans to retire next year* or *He shared some experiences from his tour of duty in Iraq.* What to replace it with? Well, um, *said* and *talked about.*

e. Qualifiers and Intensifiers

I'd estimate that three-quarters of the time, you can improve a sentence by striking out the qualifiers (*pretty, somewhat, a little, kind of,* and the currently popular *kinda, sort of, rather, arguably, slightly*) and intensifiers (*very, extremely, really, completely, totally, absolutely, unbelievably, remarkably,* and, of course, *literally*).

Qualifiers make you come off as mealymouthed.

> [*Roy Halladay is arguably the best pitcher in the National League.*]

What a weak statement! It's tantamount to saying, "I can't really back this up, but it's possible that Roy Halladay is the best pitcher in the league, maybe." Instead, pick a strong limb and take a stroll out on it:

> *Roy Halladay has the most wins, the most strikeouts, and the lowest ERA in the National League.*

> *Roy Halladay was National League managers' unanimous selection as pitcher of the year.*

Or strongest of all:

Roy Halladay is the best pitcher in the National League.

Intensifiers, meanwhile, make you seem like the Boy Who Cried Wolf: *This time they're really, really coming. I mean it! Really!* More often than not, a naked statement is stronger than one pumped up with intensifying steroids.

Transformers V *is a ~~very incredibly extremely unbelievably truly~~ bad movie.*

I don't mean to suggest that adverbs—of which qualifiers and intensifiers are examples—can't be used effectively and strategically. I just did so. The key is that *effectively* and *strategically*, in this context, are specific and precise, as opposed to adverbs meant to vaguely stoke the fire of your argument or cover your posterior.

f. Others to Avoid

- *Particular* is a currently popular four-syllable word that usually adds nothing to a thought except four syllables.

  That ~~particular~~ film is the most exciting science-fiction epic of the summer.

- *Personally* rarely if ever contributes anything of value, either.

  ~~Personally, I believe~~ U.S. tax policy is a disaster.

  (*I believe* goes as well: you wrote it, so of course you believe it.)

- *Personal* tends to be redundant, most notoriously in the expression *personal friend* (what other kinds of friends are there?), but also in:

  She led me to her ~~personal~~ office, which overlooks the museum's gardens.

- Prefacing a statement with *frankly, to tell the truth, I'm not going to lie*, or some other such pledge of verity has the effect of making you seem like you're *not* 100 percent sincere. So avoid them.

- *Actually,* a hugely popular word at the moment, is actually usually just filler.

  We ~~actually~~ met in summer camp.

- *Aforementioned* is an oddly legalistic word that has cropped up in some of my students' writing over the last few years. Why, I don't know, but I do know that it should go.

  With the publication of ~~his aforementioned novel,~~ The Corrections, *Jonathan Franzen gained a great deal of notoriety.*

- Even in quoted dialogue, stay away from dialect, or, in general, words that are spelled to indicate someone's accent or pronunciation: *kinda, gonna,* the Southerner who *laaahks* something, the *New Yawker* who *tawks like dis.* A very little of this goes a very long way. Plus, sometimes it just doesn't make sense. Sometimes a person will be described as saying, *"I wazzunt there,"* making me wonder, What, exactly, is the difference in pronunciation between *wazzunt* and *wasn't*?

2. ~~LENGTHY IS DESIRABLE~~ SHORT IS GOOD (I)

The English language is unusual and I believe unique in having thousands of pairs of synonyms in which one of the words is plain and the other fancy. Usually, the longer word is Latinate in ori-

~~purchase~~	buy	~~approximately~~	about
~~humorous~~	funny	~~require~~	need
~~possess~~	have	~~remain~~	stay
~~appears~~	seems	~~regarding~~	about
~~transpire~~	occur; happen	~~reside~~	live
~~signify~~	mean	~~principal~~	main
~~reference~~	refer to	~~definitive~~	definite
~~individual~~	person	~~frequently~~ ~~oftentimes~~	often
~~subsequently~~	later		
~~speak~~	talk	~~currently~~ ~~presently~~	now
~~lengthy~~	long		
~~utilize~~	use	~~obtain~~	get
~~signage~~	signs	~~usage~~	use
~~demonstrate~~	show	~~perhaps~~ ~~possibly~~	maybe
~~retain~~	keep		
		~~amongst~~ ~~amidst; whilst~~ ~~upon; within~~	among; amid while; on; in

gin and the shorter one Anglo-Saxon. No matter what kind of writing you're doing, it's usually the case that the simpler word is better. The chart on the previous page lists some common pairs.

You get the idea, right? Now, sometimes you will want the fancy word, for variety, ironic effect, sound, or some other reason. And hundreds and hundreds of splendid multisyllabic and/or fancy words, especially the much-maligned adjective, have no simple equivalent. What better way to describe an out-of-the-way word than *arcane,* a bitter person than *dyspeptic,* or the act of deliberately giving up something as *eschewing*? If you "own" such a word, in the sense of being confident of its meaning and nuance, go for it! (Needless to say, the best way to gain ownership of a lot of great words is to read a lot.) Otherwise, nine times out of ten, simpler is better.

E. B. White has a wonderful paragraph about his former Cornell teacher William Strunk, author of the original *Elements of Style,* which White edited and updated in the 1950s and which has been in print ever since. The subject is concise sentences (addressed in III.C.4.), rather than short words, but it is worth a listen no matter what:

> "Omit needless words!" cries the author on page 39, and into that imperative Will Strunk really put his heart and soul. In the days when I was sitting in his class, he omitted so many needless words, and omitted them so forcibly and with so much eagerness and obvious relish, that he often seemed in the position of having shortchanged himself—a man left with nothing more to say

yet with time to fill, a radio prophet who had outdis-
tanced the clock. Will Strunk got out of this predicament by a simple trick: he uttered every sentence three
times. When he delivered his oration on brevity to the
class, he leaned forward over his desk, grasped his coat
lapels in his hands and, in a husky, conspiratorial voice,
said "Rule Seventeen. Omit needless words! Omit needless words! Omit needless words!"

As I say, the passage is about short sentences, but it uses short
words. To be specific, here's the percentage of time White (generally
considered to be one of the finest American stylists of the twentieth
century) uses words of various lengths:

One-syllable: 67 percent
Two-syllable: 21 percent
Three-syllable: 10 percent
Four-syllable: 2 percent
Five-syllable: 0
Six-syllable: 1 percent
Seven-syllable or above: 0

And here, for the fun of it, is a pie chart showing the proportion
of words, by length, in the passage:

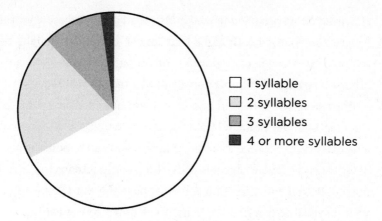

- ☐ 1 syllable
- ☐ 2 syllables
- ☐ 3 syllables
- ■ 4 or more syllables

White's proportions seem about right as a model for us all, with the understanding that there will be a little give and take in view of your own personal style and the kind of writing you're doing. Note, by the way, the three long words he used in this 128-word passage: *imperative, predicament,* and *conspiratorial.* They are eminently fine words, not replaceable by anything shorter, and a model for when it's okay to go long.

3. PRECISION: WORDS THAT ARE A BIT OFF

The online thesaurus is a great tool. The online thesaurus is a menace.

Let me expand on that thought. Three sentences ago, I used the word *tool.* If I for some reason weren't happy with it and consulted the thesaurus provided by Microsoft Word, I would be offered the following alternatives: *instrument, apparatus, implement, device, means, utensil, contrivance,* and *gizmo.* I submit that none of these would be an acceptable substitute for *tool* in that sentence, with the possible exceptions of *device* (barely) and *gizmo* (not bad).

However, if I were someone who hadn't read a lot, and especially if I were someone who thought that longer is better, I might be tempted by *instrument, apparatus, utensil,* and maybe even some others. If I gave in to temptation, I would wreck the sentence.

The thesaurus is helpful and cool if you have a strong sense of the meaning and nuance of words, and/or if you are willing and able to use the dictionary as well: that is, if you can handle the goal of writing *well*. If your object is not writing badly, it tends to get you in trouble. You will often find you don't have the word you want at your disposal. When that happens, break down your meaning into simple, short sentences of whose meaning you are completely confident. If they sound like *See Dick run,* that's okay: you can start building them back up again.

If you go through this process and find you're *still* really stuck for a word, fine, use the thesaurus. But when you have a likely candidate, take care to look it up in the dictionary. Study the definition (especially the used-in-a-sentence examples) and don't go ahead and use it until you really own the word.

Below are some examples of student sentences with off words. They have a number of other problems as well. Let's take them one by one.

> 1. [*It was these waves which took control of the stomachs of sixteen of the seventeen passengers on our boat, myself being the exception.*]

It (see III.C.6), *myself* (see III.B.1.c.), and no fewer than four prepositions (see III.C.7.) immediately jump out as trouble spots here.

The main problem in wording is *took control*, which doesn't quite work as a description of what the waves did to the stomachs. That looks ahead to the second rule in the next section: try to come up with strong subjects for sentences and clauses. *Waves* paints you into a corner when it comes to verbs.

Breaking the sentence down to its elements, you can some up with something like:

> *The waves rocked the boat, and within minutes sixteen of the seventeen passengers were seasick. I was the exception.*

If you want to keep the *waves-stomach* combination, I think the only way to go is to be a little fanciful or facetious:

> *The waves had their way with sixteen of the seventeen passengers' stomachs. I was the exception.*

> 2. [*Foreign, sour odors assaulted my nostrils, and already my stomach lurched half an inch. Giggling nervously, I tentatively pierced a large portion of kimchi with my fork, and making sure I had plenty of eerie red sauce, bit into it.*]

This is pretty good writing—specific, vivid, and active—with the exception of the two off words. Replacing *already* with *immediately* solves the first one. *Eerie* sounds like a word the thesaurus proposed to replace *strange* or *weird*. The student was right that *strange* and *weird* weren't quite right, but neither is *eerie*. What she needs is a succinct description of the sauce. I haven't tasted it, so I can't help with this one.

3. [*Walking in the front door of the café, the vestiges of domesticity are everywhere regardless of a recent remodeling.*]

Three problems: a dangling modifier (the vestiges didn't walk in the front door), the off words *vestiges* and *regardless*, and a seriously weak ending. The solution is shuffling, specificity, and trading in *vestiges* for a simpler model:

The café was remodeled last year, but when you walk in, you still see signs of domesticity everywhere.

4. [*He says the most applicable thing he learned at the university was taken from social aspect which the university provided him with.*]

Leaping out from the verbiage is the word *applicable*. One understands what's meant—that he felt he could *apply* this stuff in his later life—but that's not the way the word is properly used.

He says the most useful aspect of his time at the university was meeting and learning to live with new people.

5. [*The university's theater program has already proven to attract national media attention, not to mention it has*

*established a curriculum that makes it a staple of gradu-
ate theater in the country.]*

Number 5 is an example of typing, not writing. That is, the writer had a vague notion of what she wanted to say, put it down in a nonmindful way, and did not read it aloud with an eye to revision. I bet she had some music on and was checking her text messages. Anyway, there the sentence sits, imprecise, poorly worded, riddled with clichés and catchphrases. It actually starts out fine: the first six words are a strong subject and the beginning of a strong verb. But *already proven to* has problems in meaning and syntax; *not to mention* introduces a comma splice; *staple* is the wrong word (probably taken from the thesaurus); there's a word missing after *theater* (the writer probably deleted *program* to avoid word repetition); and *in the country* is a weak, trail-off ending.

So let's just break it down to its elements.

*The university's theater program has attracted national
media attention and established a curriculum that's the
envy of the country's other theater programs.*

Better but not great. The biggest remaining problem is the repetition of *program*. One solution is to deploy a fancy word, *counterparts*—and remember, when a fancy word is the *right* word, it doesn't present a problem.

*The university's theater program has attracted national
media attention and has a curriculum that's envied by its
counterparts throughout the country.*

4. AVOID CLICHÉS LIKE THE PLAGUE

The cliché is the poster child of bad writing.

And that, my friends, is a cliché. Clichés are bad because they're tired, overdone, unoriginal, dull, and mindless. They make you seem like everybody else, not like an individual with an interesting perspective and a voice that deserves to be listened to. But they're hard to avoid because they express a concept in a vivid and effective way (otherwise they wouldn't have become so popular), and one that the reader is sure to understand. The combination of aptness and familiarity means that clichés are constantly occurring to a writer. Some of them get excised (or exorcised) by one's internal editor, but quite a few make it to the computer screen or legal pad, where they need to be vigilantly smoked out.

Until Microsoft Word comes up with cliché-check to go along with spell-check, you'll never be able to get rid of every single one. The best you can hope for is to manage them.

To that end, it's useful to take a look at the life cycle of clichés. They are born as fresh, vivid figures of speech: often metaphors, on other occasions words or phrases used in an unexpected context. That means someone invented them. That is, a particular individual once thought to note of a not-especially-difficult enterprise, "It's not brain surgery." That was clever! The inventor deserved garlands and hosannas. Inevitably, other people started saying it as well. Over time, George Orwell observed in his classic essay "Politics and the English Language," such formulations lose "all evocative power and are merely used because they save people the trouble of inventing phrases for themselves." He dubbed them "dying metaphors," another way of saying clichés.

Orwell conceived of this as one stage, but I think there's a division within it that's worth bearing in mind. Most tempting and insidious, and thus most important to guard against, are the clichés that seem to be in the very oxygen we breathe—dying metaphors like *it's not brain surgery* and *[anything] on steroids.* Less of a problem is a category that could be called FFBC—clichés that are Famous For Being a Cliché. This would include such overworked expressions as *at the end of the day* and *it is what it is* and bromides and proverbs like *it's not the heat, it's the humidity* and *a stitch in time saves nine.* The world of sports is chock-full of these, for example, *he came to play* or *he gave 110 percent.* By this point, any conscientious writer knows these are off-limits; the vast majority of the time they come up in print is when they are mocked. (And rightfully so.)

Orwell observed that in the dying-metaphor stage, "incompatible metaphors are frequently mixed, a sure sign that the writer is not interested in what he is saying." Good point.

The *New Yorker* used to sometimes print especially egregious examples at the ends of articles, under the heading BLOCK THAT METAPHOR! Here is one published in 1989, from a letter to the *Boston Globe:*

> *In the face of mounting pressure to gut or eliminate the IRS, it continues to shoot itself in the foot by biting the hand that feeds them.*

Whew. The obvious and truly awful mixing is of hand-biting and foot-shooting, but note a phrase at the beginning of the sentence:

"mounting pressure to gut." *Pressure* and *gut* are metaphors as well, but a reader isn't likely to notice them. That's because they have arrived at the next, and final, stage of metaphorical life. After a certain number of years or decades in critical condition, a metaphor kicks the bucket and comes to seem more literal than figurative. Orwell says such a "dead metaphor . . . has in effect reverted to being an ordinary word and can generally be used without loss of vividness." When we hear of a program being *gutted*, we don't think of this as a metaphor at all and probably don't perceive it as a cliché; it's just a way of saying that the most important aspects of something were rudely removed. The same goes for referring to someone's weakness as his *Achilles' heel*, or even using a word such as *astonished,* which originally was a metaphorical suggestion of a shock so great it turned one to stone. These are okay to use, then. Just don't use too many of them, and definitely don't use more than one in the same sentence.

Here are a couple of mixed metaphors from student writing, with possible fixes.

> [*The golden age of print journalism has rusted and there is a new age emerging from the wreckage—online journalism.*]

Golden age has reached the dead metaphor stage and is (barely) acceptable; however, *wreckage* introduces a whole other idea. My approach would be to stick with the golden-age thing and actually extend it into what the poets call a *conceit*. Also, *has rusted* is kind of flat and the word *journalism* is repeated. So I would do something like:

The golden age of newspapers has turned into a pile of rust. But some smart young reporters have taken some sandpaper to it and emerged with something shiny and new—online journalism.

[*The Christian Science Reading Room is a small cove of spiritual knowledge which historically has not been a beacon of popularity among college students.*]

Small cove of spiritual knowledge isn't bad, but bringing in the *beacon* ruins the effect. I would go for something simple, just adding a little understatement at the end:

The Christian Science Reading Room is a small cove of spiritual knowledge that historically hasn't been hugely popular among college students.

A few lines up, I said it was "barely acceptable" to use dead metaphors. If I don't seem enthusiastic, that's because, first, even a cliché which doesn't smell bad anymore smells worse than something fresh, and, second, in a particular case, some people might feel it's not dead yet (as Monty Python would put it), that it's still a cliché. The bottom line is the importance of at least developing an awareness of the sell-by date on words and expressions, weighing them in your mind, and acting judiciously. (In that sentence, I used three metaphors: *bottom line, sell-by date,* and *weighing.* I decided that they were dead, not dying. What do you think?)

I'd like to add another stage Orwell didn't think of, perhaps because he didn't live in the Internet era, when everything, including clichés' lives, moves much faster than it ever did before. In today's highly interactive world, there is a period—between the invention of a metaphor and the point at which it is definitively arrived at cliché land—in which it's not only usable but can be lively and fun.

Consider the expression *[to] throw [someone] under the bus,* meaning to publicly betray an erstwhile ally. The earliest use I have been able to find is a 1994 quote from a *Pittsburgh Post-Gazette* article: "Bethel Park council is delaying action on a site plan for an ice arena because of legal action by a citizens group opposing the project. Council president Philip Ehrman said the group is 'trying to throw the community under the bus.'" It first showed up in the *New York Times* in 2000, but didn't really take off till a few years later, with seven uses in 2005 and thirteen in 2006—including, crucially, a discussion in William Safire's "On Language" column in November. Up until that point, I would submit, *throw under the bus* was a still-new toy with which writers could give readers some shared pleasure. This is a risky business, however, because different people will have different notions on where a particular phrase lies at a particular point in time.

There's one more strategy for making a cliché acceptable: the old switcheroo. In 1937, *Time* magazine observed, "To the people who voted for him last November, Franklin Roosevelt was Mr. Right." Since roughly that time, *Mr. Right*—meaning a male who is perfect husband material—has been a cliché. One strategy for making it (marginally) acceptable was *Time*'s: that is, using it in a political as opposed to romantic context. There matters stood until 1985, when a television movie called *Romance on the Orient Express* contained this piece of dialogue: "I'm not looking for Mr. Right, I'm looking for Mr. Right Now." Good show! The screenwriter tweaked the cliché and made it usable again. By now, of course, *Mr. Right Now* is as clichéd as it gets—and so is a recent (unisex) replacement, *The One.* Yet another variation would be needed to remove the stigma: *Mr. Write* for a dreamy literary guy, *Mr. Left* if the woman demanded a mate with progressive politics, *Mr. Far Right* for folks on the other end of the spectrum, *Mr. Righter* for someone chosen over a current beau, *Mr. Rite Aid* for a hypochondriac, *Mr. Wry* for an ironic sort, and so forth. You get the idea.

Even beyond the fact that the target is moving ~~at warp speed~~ extremely fast, it is impossible to provide a comprehensive list of clichés. First, there are way too many of them. Second, especially on the margins between dead and dying, what's a cliché to you may not be one to me: it's an inherently subjective judgment. Third, clichés are field-specific: if you are immersed in the world of sports, or pop music, or business, or higher education, you will be highly sensitized to particular buzzwords and catchphrases that would strike a layperson as unremarkable or unintelligible. And finally, they are register-specific. That is, a cliché in the world of blogs will not be one in the world of scholarly journals, and vice versa.

That being said, here's a brief list of words and phrases that in my judgment are currently clichés and thus are to be avoided in writing:

That being said
Iconic
Viral
Curate
Deal breaker
Difference maker

The decider
Heavy lifting
High-maintenance
Perfect storm
Brick and mortar
Tsunami
It is what it is
Surreal
The [choose letter of the alphabet]-word
Not so much (as in *I like him. Her? Not so much*).
McMansions, McJobs, etc.
[Anything] on steroids
Bucket list
Kerfuffle
Badass
Spoiler alert
The Man (as in *working for*)
Back in the day
Not your father's [anything]
Really? (to indicate skepticism)
Artisanal
Plated
House-made
Kick the can down the road
Meme
[anything] 2.0
Man-kini, man-cave, man-date, manorexia, or
    man-anything else

Get off my lawn!
Now get off my lawn!

5. EUPHEMISM, BUZZWORDS, AND JARGON

These closely related categories resemble clichés in being (as Tom and Ray of the radio show *Car Talk* like to say) unencumbered by the thought process. Euphemisms are prettifying terms. The classic example is the collection of ever-more-euphemistic words for the place where one goes to *relieve oneself*, which itself is a euphemism for *urinate* or *defecate*.* Thus we say *restroom*, which is a euphemism for *men's room* or *ladies' room*, which is a euphemism for *bathroom*, which is a euphemism for *toilet*, which is a euphemism for *privy*, which is a euphemism for . . . well, this notion is apparently so horrible and unpleasant that we don't have an actual word for it. I guess that if there were a need to refer to it in writing, I would recommend *bathroom* as the most straightforward, even though baths are rarely taken there.

The military is famously a fount of euphemism, with such terms as *armed intervention* (war), *neutralize* (kill), *pacify* (kill), *collateral damage* (unintentionally kill), *friendly fire* (unintentionally kill fellow soldiers), and *enhanced interrogation* (torture). Euphemisms for pregnancy are legion as well. The most recent term I'm aware of

---

* It could be argued that those terms are themselves pseudo-clinical euphemisms for four-letter words beginning with *p* and *s*. I leave that determination to wiser heads than mine.

originated in Great Britain in the 1990s and has been taken up by American celebrity journalists with a vengeance; it is to refer to a pregnant woman as having a *baby bump*.

Need I say that, unless you're being ironic or quoting someone, *enhanced interrogation, baby bump*, and their ilk should not pass through your fingers?

Jargon—instances of which are sometimes known as *buzzwords*—differs from euphemism in a couple of ways. It usually originated with members of a particular occupation or group, and it usually fancifies or obfuscates something that doesn't have an especially negative connotation. Sometimes, it names a thing or phenomenon for which there was no previous word. Sometimes, it means pretty much nothing at all. Jargon is a more egregious problem than euphemism, in my experience; it is strangely enticing and can spread like a virus.

Politics is home to a particular kind of jargon: words and phrases intended to spin a particular issue in a particular direction. People on different sides of the political spectrum express the same concepts in completely different vocabularies! Thus *progressives* are *pro-choice* and in favor of *investment* and increasing *revenue*. *Patriotic Americans,* for their part, rail against *abortion on demand, tax-and-spend policies*, the *death tax,* and *the Democrat Party*. (The last is a clever one, in subtly dissociating the party with small-*d democratic*.) If you're on one side or the other and trying to stoke the fire on any of these issues, go nuts with the terms I've used and the many others like them. However, if your aim is to write in an intelligent, nonpartisan way, avoid them at all costs. Instead, seek words that accurately and temperately convey meaning, such as *legalized abortion, government spending, taxes* (in general), and *the estate tax* (in particular).

Prose that comes from business—both advertising and public relations, on the one hand, and internal communication, on the other—contains more jargon than nonjargon. The particular terms in vogue change from time to time. Currently, they include *reach out to* (contact or get in touch with), *going forward* (in the future), *monetize* (make money from), *best practices* (doing something in a good or efficient way), *sustainable* (doing something so as not to degrade *the environment*, which itself is a buzzword that made its way into general diction), *grow* (transitive verb meaning "develop" or "increase the size of"), *give back* (make a charitable contribution or conduct a charitable enterprise), *bandwidth* (personal or organizational capacity), and *rightsize* (save money by firing people—which takes us back to euphemism).

Between writing that paragraph and this one, I had lunch and read the *New York Times*, which reported that a radio corporation called Clear Channel Communications had fired several dozen disk jockeys employed by the radio stations it owns around the country. The *Times* quoted "a company spokeswoman" as saying: "We've completely rethought our regional market strategy and reinvented our operations in those markets in a way that will let us compete on a new level—and succeed using all of Clear Channel's resources, scale and talent."

That is euphemistic jargon on a very high level indeed. If you work and write for a business, or if you aspire to, you might want to study it, for a mastery of this discourse seems to be essential if you want to rise to the top. I certainly hope the student who wrote the following sentence for one of my journalism classes was interested in a career in public relations or corporate communications, rather than as an actual writer, trying to tell something true to actual readers:

> [*The employer relation's team at Career Services has made a strong effort in trying to facilitate an assertive outreach program toward alumni in order to help build a better partnership with alumni and current students.*]

Actually, that's probably a bit much even in a business setting. In any case, what he meant to say was:

> *The employer relations department at Career Services has asked alumni to get in touch with students.*

Generally speaking, this kind of nonsense isn't that hard to avoid. But somewhat more insidious is a collection of terms that originated, I believe, in psychology and other *helping professions* (itself a prime bit of jargon). The two worst offenders are the verb *share* (often used as a synonym for *say,* as in *He shared that he was coming home*) and the noun *issues* used to mean *problems* or *disagreements* or some other negative feelings, as in *She has issues with her mother.* My closing piece of advice in this section—and words to live by in general—is to write, when the facts support it:

> *She despises her mother.*

C. Sentences

1. WORD REP.

The above phrase (the second part of which is an abbreviation for *repetition*) is the comment I write most frequently on student papers. That's because, I think, word repetition is a telltale—maybe *the* telltale—sign of awkward, nonmindful writing. The writer has presumably gotten the pertinent information onto the screen or page, but has not taken the time to read the sentence to herself, silently or out loud. If she did, that word rep. would sound like a fingernail on the blackboard. Consequently, "listening" to your sentences with the sensitivity and skill to pick up word repetition is a strong first step toward mindful writing.

There are some nuances to my unified theory of word repetition, which boil down to: the more common the word, the more leeway you have in repeating it, and vice versa. In the previous sentence, I repeated *to, word, more,* and *the* (twice!). That is not ideal, but it's okay; readers are not likely to notice. On the other hand, I know I have to wait at least a few more pages before reusing *nuances, leeway,* or the expressions *vice versa* and *boils down to.* Words like *repetition* and *common* would be somewhere in between. I would not be able to use the notion of *unified theory* again in the entire article or book.

The word-repetition problem can be hard to solve. Usually, a writer uses a word twice because no alternative is self-evident or, sometimes, conceivable after what seems like a lengthy period of cogitation. A particular pitfall is the infelicity that H. M. Fowler dubbed *elegant variation.* He was referring to a synonym, near synonym, or invented synonym used for the express and blatant purpose of avoiding word repetition.

For example (EV in brackets):

> *Hartnell read the newspaper. When he was finished [with the periodical], he got up and went outside.*

> *Spence hit a home run in the second inning, his fifth [circuit clout] of the campaign.*

In these cases, as is often true, the simplest solution is simply to take the EV out. Voilà! Incidentally, perceptive readers may have noticed that the second sentence contains another EV: *the campaign.* Mediocre sportswriters are elegant variers to the bone, and they will reflexively seek to avoid a common word, in this case *season.* However, *season* is better than *campaign.*

Back to word repetition, check out these examples from student work, with the repeated word underlined. First make sure you read them attentively enough to notice that the repetition is unfortunate. Below each sentence I'll suggest a fix.

> [*Spending the day rushing from Memorial Hall to Main Street to Trabant is a typical <u>day</u> at the University of Delaware.*]

Pretty easy.

> *A typical day at the University of Delaware involves rushing from Memorial Hall to Main Street to Trabant.*

Improving this one doesn't involve much heavy lifting, either.

[*When I was an undergraduate student earning a minor in painting I developed a particular interest in de Kooning's __paintings__.*]

When I was an undergraduate earning a minor in painting, I developed a particular interest in de Kooning's work.

Here's one that's easier still:

[*Johnson is the youngest representative in the legislature. When he was twenty-three, __Johnson__ defeated the Republican incumbent.*]

For some reason, many writers tend to needlessly repeat proper names, apparently forgetting that at their disposal are the very useful pronouns *he* and *she*—which have the added value of being the category of common words, mentioned above, that can be repeated with near impunity.

Johnson is the youngest representative in the legislature. At twenty-three, he defeated the Republican incumbent.

Moving to something a little more challenging, here's one that requires some mindful pruning. (Note, in passing, the use of the passive voice. It's a problem in the original because, among other reasons, the identity of "they" is not given. But contrary to what's often written, the passive can be effective, and I think it is in the revision.)

> [*During the journey children were abducted and taken into captivities where they turned the boys into child soldiers carrying guns twice the size of the young boys.*]

> *During the journey, the boys were abducted, taken into captivity, and turned into soldiers carrying guns twice their size.*

Sometimes, writers seem to develop a repetition compulsion regarding a particular word:

> [*Whether they are nice robots like Rosie the robot maid in the Jetsons, C3PO in Star Wars; or mean robots like the robot overlords in the Matrix, robots are a steady figure in popular culture.*]

Whew. Robot much? I think my approach to this would be to embrace the repetition, somewhat, specifically going from five iterations to three, and meanwhile fixing the punctuation and changing that phrase *steady figure.* So it would become:

> *Whether they are nice robots like Rosie the maid in* The Jetsons *and C3PO in* Star Wars, *or mean robots like the overlords in* The Matrix, *robots are recurring figures in popular culture.*

(Or you could just take out every *robot* except the last one. Your choice.)

Here's an insider's tip. Take a look at the example I gave a few paragraphs up, the one about de Kooning. Did anybody notice I replaced *paintings* with *work*? Well, I did, and I maintain that even though it's a substituted word, it's not elegant variation. The trick is, when there's no readily apparent way to avoid repetition, it often works to find a word referring to a broader or narrower category of the first one. So *painting/work* is okay (broader), as is *painting/ neo-expressionistic portraits* (narrower). But *paintings/canvases* is elegant variation.

2. START STRONG

Here is the most underrated writing tip I know: when possible, make the subject of a sentence a person, a collection of persons, or a thing. When you choose a concept or some other intangible as a subject, you're generally forced into an awkward verb or, at best, the passive voice.

> [*Intelligence is a quality shared by every member of the family.*]

> *Everybody in the family is smart.*

> [*Benefits an organization gains when reusing water include sustainability, good publicity, great economic incentives, and good relations with water conservation programs, said Huang.*]

Huang said that when an organization reuses water, it gains many benefits: sustainability, publicity, economic incentives, and good relations with water conservation programs.

———————

[Qualities such as imagination and engagement are qualities the admissions board ways heavily.]

Qualities such as those *qualities; ways* instead of *weighs.* Hard as it may be to believe, I certify this is an actual student sentence. Anyweigh, I mean anyway:

The admissions board is always on the lookout for qualities like imagination and engagement.

———————

[Unusual flavor pairings are what best characterize Chef Juan Garces' restaurants.]

Chef Juan Garces is known for pairing unusual flavors.

The following three-sentence excerpt from an article about a city council meeting is a symphony of weak openings. And by the way, either that is a spell-check error in the first sentence or it was an extraordinarily tense meeting.

[The opening of the meeting was similar to past openings with mediation and the pledge of allegiance. Applause

was loud when Mayor Funk hugged and congratulated Rose Gallante, Anita Hunter, Harry McKenry, Judy Miller, and finally Euretta Schultheiss on their contributions to the Newark Police Department. The years of dedication ranged from three years of service to eighteen.]

The meeting opened with the customary moment of silent meditation followed by the Pledge of Allegiance. Mayor Funk congratulated Rose Gallante, Anita Hunter, Harry McKenry, Judy Miller, and Euretta Schultheiss on their service—ranging from three to eighteen years—to the Newark Police Department. As he was hugging them, spectators erupted into thunderous applause.

3. END STRONG

[*Having a strong ending is as important as having a strong beginning for a sentence.*]

I hope you see how the sentence above—while being grammatically correct, precise, and relatively concise—violates the very maxim it offers, and as a result ends up as weak as the beer at a college mixer.

Unfortunately, a great many of our first-draft sentences seem to want to end with a whimpering trail of prepositional phrases, nonessential details, and other extraneous material. One word for this is *anticlimax.* Once you've recognized the problem—a key step, as always—the first thing to do is figure out which word represents the most important idea, then see if you can make this the *last* word. In the example, it was pretty easy to figure out that this magic word was *ending* and to shove it to the end:

> *Possibly the most important principle in constructing sentences is having a strong ending.*

You usually won't go wrong if you end with a direct object. Concluding prepositional phrases are unavoidable, to a certain extent, but never double or triple them. Thus *The priest went back to his homeland* is fine, but not *The priest went back to his homeland after his vacation*. To fix that one, how about:

> *After his vacation, the priest went back to his homeland.*

It's not always that simple. Consider:

> 1. [*He's going to attack a lot of these problems about global warming in the future.*]

> 2. [*The winner of the lottery was an employee of the firm named Henry Galston.*]

> 3. [*In a flurry we grabbed some plastic containers filled with sprouts and kimchi, spending about $12.75 on these ingredients for dinner.*]

One helpful strategy for the first two is, rather than look for the most important concept, to take almost the opposite tack: gather together the trailing-off stuff and front-load it, either at the beginning of the sentence or before key nouns and verbs. By the way, both 1 and 2 are not only weak but have ambiguity problems. In 1, are we talking about future problems or a future attack?; and in 2, a reader briefly wonders if this firm might conceivably be called Henry Galston.

After front-loading, number 1 becomes:

> *In the future, he's going to attack a lot of these global-warming problems.*

Number 2 is better served by flipping the whole thing around:

> *An employee named Henry Galston won the lottery.*

The third sentence, meanwhile, is better served by being cut in two:

> *In a flurry we grabbed some plastic containers filled with sprouts and kimchi. The damages were $12.75.*

Much more often than not, you will want your last word to be a noun. I just took a look at a "Talk of the Town" piece by a good *New Yorker* writer named Nick Paumgarten ("Big Picture," July 11 and 18, 2011) and calculated that (not counting quotations), thirty-nine of the forty-five sentences in it end with nouns, pronouns, or proper names. All of these are either direct objects (as in the second sentence in the following passage) or the object of prepositional phrases (as in the first). The article is about a newfangled Polaroid camera, which is operated by a woman named Jennifer Trausch:

The strobe flash made a loud pop, and Trausch began slowly pulling the paper through the machine. She laid the print on the table and after ninety seconds peeled back the protective layer to reveal a stately black-and-white image edged in a chemical sludge they call "goop."

Of the six non-noun-ending sentences in the article—all of which are good sentences, by the way—four end with verbs and two with adjectives. An example of the first category is a long sentence that discusses Polaroid enthusiasts' efforts ". . . to try to make new film, using different chemicals and processes, since the old ones were environmentally hazardous or difficult to duplicate."

An example of the second (referring to the director Oliver Stone, three photos of whom were taken with the camera) is: "Stone and the camera crew stood over them, trying to choose which was best."

Going through the other parts of speech, you will never (except for stunts) end a sentence with an article or conjunction. Adverbs can work when it's the adverb you're stressing:

He played relentlessly and well.

That leaves prepositions. In the last chapter, I said it's not in fact true that you can't end a sentence with a preposition. However, you normally shouldn't, because prepositions are so often weak that you could make the case they are inherently so. Consider:

[*Abernathy lives in the neighborhood the cougar was found in.*]

Yuck—and note the repetition of *in*. The fix that will usually first come to mind involves the word *which,* which leads in this case to:

> [*Abernathy lives in the neighborhood in which the cougar was found.*]

That's not so good, either. It's wordy, and pretty obvious you're trying to avoid a preposition at the end. The way to go here is to flip things around:

> *The cougar was found in Abernathy's neighborhood.*

To be sure, prepositions can work as endings. You just have to take each sentence on its merits.

> *What in God's name are you talking about?*

> *I wish those cougars would go back where they came from.*

> *Don't come in.*

4. ~~LENGTHY IS DESIRABLE~~ SHORT IS GOOD (II)

Early in this part, I talked about using the shortest word that expresses your meaning and used a passage from *The Elements of Style* to illustrate the point. The same is true of sentences. Here is a famous passage from the original edition of the book, published as a pamphlet by William Strunk in 1918, in which Strunk explains what he means by the motto "Omit needless words":

Vigorous writing is concise. A sentence should contain no unnecessary words, a paragraph no unnecessary sentences, for the same reason that a drawing should have no unnecessary lines and a machine no unnecessary parts. This requires not that the writer make all his sentences short, or that he avoid all detail and treat his subjects only in outline, but that every word tell.

Frankly, I am not so wild about Strunk's use of the words *unnecessary* and *needless*. They wrongly imply, it seems to me, that there is one right way to express any particular thought, and that the way to achieve it is just to pare away all extraneous words until you get there. But I get what he means and I certainly concur with the sentiment "Vigorous [or "not-bad"] writing is concise." I like his acknowledgment that a good long sentence can be very cool. And I love his use of the old-fashioned verb *tell* (in the old-fashioned subjunctive voice, no less). In a not-bad sentence, every word is serving a purpose. You should be able to identify what that purpose is. A good deal of revision involves going over your sentences and identifying words that *aren't* serving a purpose and, as Strunk would say, omitting them.

Writing concisely is both selfish and generous. It's generous because it contains an implicit acknowledgment that the reader's time is valuable and that you do not intend to waste it. It's selfish because, compared to verbosity, it is a much more effective way to get your point across.

Admittedly, it takes a good deal of time and effort to achieve. It's much easier to write long than to write short. You could call it the Dickens Fallacy: somehow, we all seem to have an ingrained sense that we're being paid by the word. Once you get that excessive sentence down, then examining it for those needless words is laborious in itself. And when you've spotted them, you generally can't just pluck them out and be done with it; the sentence has to be reshaped. But all this has always been the case.

Below are some pieces of verbosity from students' work, with edits.

> [*The book compiles fifty-two pieces of work from forty-five different writers each and every one of whom has a special connection to the tiny state of Delaware.*]

> *The book has fifty-two pieces of work from forty-five writers, each with a Delaware connection.*

> ———————

> [*Cromartie hopes students leave the presentations with a better appreciation and understanding of the people of Uganda, the strife they are living with daily and the impoverished conditions from which they are trying to rise above through the education of children and vocational training for adults.*]

> *Cromartie said he hoped students would leave the presentations with a better understanding of both the people of Uganda and the efforts they're making to improve the terrible conditions there.*

> ———————

> [*City council members expressed inspections are to insure the healthy living environments residing within rental*

properties as well as to protect the city from future incidents.]

That one combines wordiness with vagueness. It's missing information, and I have used my poetic license to provide it.

Two city council members made the point that inspections are important, both to promote the health of residents and to protect the city from lawsuits.

————————

[*In an age that could not have even anticipated news being spread via the Internet, broadcast journalism took the media world by storm and allowed reporters to pledge their allegiance through trustworthy pieces aimed to satisfy the public interest.*]

In the 1950s and '60s, broadcast journalism became more popular and effective.

————————

[*Not only do journalists possess an undying passion to uncover and showcase relevant information to enhance the public's knowledge on current events, but exhibit a willingness to go to great lengths to obtain stories fit to print.*]

The best journalists are passionate about their work and indefatigable in tracking down stories.

5. THE PERILS OF AMBIGUITY

a. Crash Blossoms

In a *New York Times Magazine* "On Language" column in 2010, Ben Zimmer described how Mike O'Connell, an American editor based in Japan, was bemused by an article in a local newspaper about the successful musical career of a young musician whose father had died in a 1985 Japan Airlines plane crash. Specifically, he was bothered by the headline—VIOLINIST LINKED TO JAL CRASH BLOSSOMS—which made him wonder, "What's a crash blossom?" O'Connell and another editor, Dan Bloom, thereupon coined *Crash Blossoms* as a term for such vexingly ambiguous headlines. Zimmer listed some prime examples:

[MCDONALD'S FRIES THE HOLY GRAIL FOR POTATO FARMERS]

[BRITISH LEFT WAFFLES ON FALKLANDS]

[GATOR ATTACKS PUZZLE EXPERTS]

And two all-time greats, used by the *Columbia Journalism Review* for its collections of misleading headlines:

[SQUAD HELPS DOG BITE VICTIM]

[RED TAPE HOLDS UP NEW BRIDGE]

The classic Crash Blossom is born out of the compression demanded by headlines, and the confusion can often be eliminated by adding missing words or changing the verb from present tense to something more appropriate:

MCDONALD'S FRIES ARE THE HOLY GRAIL . . .

THE BRITISH LEFT IS WAFFLING . . .

ALLIGATOR ATTACKS ARE PUZZLING EXPERTS

b. If Only English Were German

But Crash Blossoms are not limited to headlines. The English language has a lot of tricks up its sleeve, and once a sentence gets beyond a "See Dick run" level of complexity, the ordering of the elements within it takes on a crucial strategic importance. As E. B. White observed, sometimes trying to cogently set down a thought requires "sheer luck, like getting across the street." Certainly, ambiguity is a frequent problem in my students' prose. Below, some of their sentences are grammatically correct but ambiguous if not misleading because of the way the elements of the sentence are ordered; snarky (mis)interpretations follow.

1. [*I went back to visit the house I grew up in last week.*]

Growing up in a week is a pretty neat trick.

2. [*Ashley finished painting the new garage door that she put up yesterday this morning.*]

Wait, did she put up the door yesterday or this morning?

3. [*Gannett is sponsoring a panel about blogging in the Perkins Auditorium.*]

What about blogging *outside* the Perkins Auditorium?

4. [*Lincoln University has dropped its controversial three-year-old requirement that students must take an exercise class with a Body Mass Index greater than 30.*]

Weird-sounding class.

5. [*We saw the film that won the Oscar and went home.*]

And where exactly does the film live?

6. [*[Bert] Blyleven . . . a wily veteran with a wicked curve-ball who was finishing a twenty-two-year career with the California Angels.*]

That's some career for a curveball. (The above quote was taken from the *New York Times*).

7. [*I smile to see my Christmas stocking still hanging on the fireplace, and smell a savory, homemade ravioli dinner escaping the kitchen stove.*]

I hope you didn't have cleanup duties that night. Ravioli can be messy.

>8. [*She has on authentic Native American moccasins made directly from Navajo women.*]

Ouch.

>9. [*Last night I shot an elephant in my pajamas.*]

How he got in my pajamas, I don't know. (The above quote and rejoinder were both uttered by Groucho Marx in the film *Animal Crackers,* written by George S. Kaufman and Morrie Ryskind.)

As the Groucho quote indicates, verbal ambiguity is at the root of a lot of humor, some of it funny and some not very. But if you're just trying to get your point across, this is a problem. Fortunately, in most cases, the problem can be addressed and resolved simply by reading aloud, or, more generally, mindfulness. If, every time you put down a sentence, you go over it unhurriedly, you'll learn to pick up on any ambiguities or confusion. To fix them, just shuffle and reshuffle the elements of the sentence, as if you were putting together a bouquet of flowers. Eventually, you'll come up with more than one reasonable and pleasing alternative, from which you can choose the one you like best.

Interestingly, the confusions in the above examples all stem from the same basic problem. A noun (A) is followed and modified by a relative clause or prepositional phrase (B) and then by another element (C). This appears to be a particular calamity in English, in which nouns are largely uninflected (that is, they take the same form whether they are subjects or objects) and modifying or descriptive phrases *have* to come after the noun. Friends who're more knowledgeable than I tell me that in German and ancient Greek, you can create a construction along the lines of "about-blogging panel" or "wily, with-a-wicked-curveball veteran" or "in-my-pajamas I."

In English, you have to move stuff. In the first three examples, the problem is the placement of the time (1 and 2) and place (3) elements. By shifting them around, I came up with:

> *Last week, I visited the house I grew up in.*

> *Ashley put up a new garage door yesterday; she has to paint it by tonight.*

> *Gannett is sponsoring a panel about blogging, to be held in the Perkins Auditorium.*

In example 4, the trouble stems from breaking up a noun phrase, rarely a good idea:

> *Lincoln University has dropped a controversial three-year-old rule requiring students with a Body Mass Index of 30 or more to take an exercise class.*

And in 5, the problem is confusion over which of two nouns—*we* or *the film*—belongs with the verb *went.*

> *We saw the Oscar-winning film, then went home.*

Number 6 becomes *a wily veteran, known for his wicked curveball, who was finishing a twenty-two-year career*... Wait! I just found another misleading thing about the sentence! Blyleven played for five different teams, not just the Angels. So let's make it ... *a wily veteran, known for his wicked curveball, who was pitching for the Angels, the last stop in his twenty-two-year career.*

The last one I almost hate to fix, because it so brutally drains the humor out of a classic line, but that's why they pay me the medium bucks. So apologies to Groucho, and here goes:

> *Last night, while I was wearing my pajamas, I shot an elephant.*

6. WHAT IS THE WHAT? OR, THE TROUBLE WITH VAGUE PRONOUNS

a. Who He?

A mindful writer tracks his or her antecedents and tidies up the campsite to make sure there isn't any ambiguity.

> [*Raymond met Chris Bruce while he was attending the boot camp as YouDee in 1998.*]

I can't correct it because I don't know if Raymond or Chris was attending the camp as YouDee (which, or who, is the mascot of the University of Delaware). If R., then it could be, *Raymond met Chris Bruce while attending the boot camp as YouDee.* If C.B., then I would write, *Raymond met Chris Bruce while Bruce was attending...*

b. There Is/There Are

We all are fond of the expressions *there is* and *there are* because they come naturally and often seem to fit whatever bill needs fitting, but they lead to limp sentences. Following the logic of item III.C.2., if a sentence with a weak subject is bad, a sentence starting with *There are* is even worse—it doesn't even *have* a subject.

Fortunately, a fix is usually pretty easy. A lot of the time, you just get rid of the *There are* and a relative pronoun (*who*, *that*), and voilà. For example, *There are five poets who have given readings at the school this year* becomes *Five poets have given readings at the school this year.*

My rule of thumb is that *there-are* constructions are okay if you can replace the *is* or *are* with *exists* or *exist*. E.g.: *There are twenty-five three-star restaurants in Rome.* Not only does that work, but trying to change it forces you to use verbs that come off as trying much too hard, e.g., *Twenty-five three-star restaurants grace Rome* or *Rome is host to twenty-five three-star restaurants.*

It takes just a little bit more work when, as is often the case, *there* is a blanket thrown over some unsightly vagueness.

> [*In terms of this coming year for entering freshman there has been a question of difficulty of difficulty of entry for out-of-state students.*]

> *Compared to last year, the Admissions Office selected a lower percentage of out-of-state applicants for admission in the fall.*

> [*Lieutenant Brian Henry explained that there are spe-cific jurisdictional agreements associated with the New-ark Police Department and campus police.*]

I can't fix that one because I don't know what the "specific juris-dictional agreements" are. And without knowing that, you cannot write a not-bad sentence on the subject.

c. It

The eighteenth-century English writer William Cobbett called *it* "the greatest troubler that I know of in language. It is so small, and so convenient, that few are careful enough in using it." One of the troubles is ambiguity, as in these examples:

> [*When it comes down to it, students enjoy spending a little time at home, with* little *being the key word.*]

> *Students enjoy spending a little time at home, with* little *being the key word.*

> _____

> [*While it seems like a good idea in theory, many students are concerned about the future possibility of not having a car on campus if it becomes too expensive.*]

> *Having a car on campus seems like a good idea in theory, but it often ends up being just too expensive.*

[*In his speech about the first year of his administration, President Harker said it is no longer acceptable to go it alone.*]

In his speech, President Harker said the university could no longer afford to act alone.

Even when the meaning is clear, *it* spawns limp writing and wordiness.

[*It is hard to play the guitar as fast as Clapton.*]

Playing guitar as fast as Clapton is hard.

———————

[*It is true that the Democrats lost many House seats in 2010, but it's also true that they still control the Senate.*]

Although the Democrats lost many House seats in 2010, they still control the Senate.

d. This, That, and the Other

This is an indispensable word in movie titles (what would the Billy Crystal–Robert De Niro movie series do without it?) and in conversation, where, to me, it gives the impression of the speaker brandishing something held in his or her hands. However, most writing books recommend extreme caution when using *this* in print, especially naked. For the most part, I agree. In writing, you don't have the use of your hands, and the word just sits there, often raising more questions than it resolves. A student wrote:

> [*In 1827, following a furious debate in Parliament, in which each party made an eloquent case and the Prime Minister resigned, slavery was outlawed. This had an immediate effect on the country's politics.*]

I circled the word *This,* drew a line to the margin, and wrote in big letters, "WHAT?" That is, was the writer referring to the debate, the cases made by the parties, the resignation, or the new law? My hunch is that she didn't really know, and used *this* to mean, basically, "all the stuff I just said." That is not not-bad writing.

Here's a reliable tip. As in the previous sentence, *that* often comes off as a little more precise and forceful than *this,* so it can be slipped in without doing any damage. You didn't hear it from me.

e. What

Starting a sentence or dependent clause with *what* is usually a form of throat clearing and ersatz suspense that really just creates wordiness and an unnecessary use of the verb *to be.* Moreover, *what* is singular, and so in cases where it stands for a plural (as in the first example below), awkward conjugation choices ensue.

> [*What this university needs ~~are~~ is better professors.*]

> *This university needs better professors.*

[*What he wanted to stress was that credit cards are dangerous.*]

He stressed that credit cards are dangerous.

7. WHEN YOU CATCH A PREPOSITION, KILL IT

Pardon me for paraphrasing the title of one of my books, which I stole from Mark Twain: "When you catch an adjective, kill it." Adjectives can indeed be a problem. They are the prime culprits of telling-not-showing, which I feel is the single biggest general prose misstep. They can be wordy and sleep inducing, especially when mashed together in pairs or triplets.

But in my experience, prepositions are worse. Prepositions, of course, are the part of speech indicating relationship: *in, of, to, with, from, under, over,* and so on. They are absolutely necessary, but they are inherently weak and often imprecise. Calling someone *a person with plans* or *a man of his word* leaves so much open to speculation! Moreover, after a certain point, prepositions turn a sentence into a drawn-out blah. They actually do bring a sort of rhythm with them, but it's an unfortunate, numbing rhythm, the anapest. This is the duh-duh-DUM-duh-duh-DUM of limericks and "'Twas the *night* before *Christ*mas and *all* through the *house*." Lastly, prepositions are also often the perpetrators of the sorts of ambiguities and confusion described previously in the book.

My general rule is to allow one preposition per sentence, or two at the most. Any more than that and you have to cast an extremely cold eye.

The problem is, prepositions flow so naturally out of one's fingers! As proof that they happen to the best of us, I give you a sentence—part of a review of a reality show called *Sweet Home Alabama*—by Ginia Bellafante, a TV critic for the *New York Times* and one of the top writers at the paper. (I've underlined the prepositions.)

> [*Here Devin, a pretty, blond student <u>in</u> a cowboy hat <u>at</u> the University <u>of</u> Alabama, is made to select <u>from</u> 20 bachelors, 10 <u>of</u> them "country," and the rest mostly <u>from</u> the Northeast or Los Angeles.*]

How to fix? Well, of the six prepositions, the real culprits are the first two, *in* and *at;* they, and the unfortunate prepositional phrases they initiate, trail behind Devin like a pair of tired, shambling dogs. The last three are innocuous, though the repetition of *from* isn't ideal. I'm also struck that the sentence is pretty long. So . . .

> *Devin, a pretty, blond University of Alabama student who is almost always seen in a cowboy hat, is made to select from 20 bachelors. Half are "country," and half come from Los Angeles or the Northeast.*

Better, right? A description of how often she is shown in a cowboy hat (which I admittedly made up) is funnier, more precise, and more vivid than the vague *in.* The transplanted U of Alabama reference illustrates the way you can often strengthen a sentence by rejiggering a prepositional phrase and putting it before the noun.

Thus *The owner of the shop* becomes *The shop's owner* or *The shop owner; a guy with a bald head* becomes *a bald guy.*

As I said, English is not German, where complex and endless adjectives can be constructed, so sometimes you have to figure out exactly how a string of prepositions can be condensed.

> [*I said hello to a friend with a T-shirt with a picture of Bart Simpson on the front.*]

> *I said hello to a friend in a Bart Simpson T-shirt.*

8. TO USE *TO BE* OR NOT TO USE *TO BE*

a. Abstract Nouns

Preposition abuse is often linked to a couple of other weak sisters of language: the verbs *to be* (often in the form of the passive voice) or *to have,* the definite article (that is, *the*), and abstract nouns, especially ones ending in *-tion.* The problem is especially vexing in my field, academia. But you also find it in government, business, and various other outposts of bureaucracy, where passing the buck and generally not saying what you mean is valued. In this (admittedly extreme) example, abstract nouns are in **bold,** *to be* verbs in [brackets], *the*s in *italics,* and prepositions underlined.

> Going forward, *the* **solution** to *the* **dissatisfaction** [will be] a **reconsideration** of *the* **initiative** that [was] offered by *the* **administration.**

(I threw in a current cliché, *going forward,* just for fun.)

So much mealymouthed dancing around the subject, so little meat. The point, such as it is, seems to be:

> *Students have made it clear that they hate the new policy,*
> *so the administration will change it.*

Here's a simple two-part way of sussing out if a *to be* verb is a problem.

1. If the back half of the sentence takes the form *to be* + *possessive/article/identifier* + *noun* or *to be* + *adjective*, you're probably okay. Using song titles again, that would give you:

   We are the world.

   The song is you.

   You're the top.

   The lady is a tramp.

   The gentleman is a dope.

   I am the walrus.

   You are so beautiful.

   We are family.

2. However, if the sentence takes the form *noun* + *to be* + *prepositional phrase* or *to be* + *noun* + *who/that/which* + *verb phrase*, there's a strong chance it could be beefed up, usually with a stronger and more specific verb. For example:

[*Obama is the beneficiary of the union's donations.*]

The union gave money to Obama.

[*Rizzotti is the student who won this year's citizenship award.*]

Rizzotti won this year's citizenship award.

b. The Passive Can Be Used, but Not Always

Don't use the passive voice is one of those rules—like *change "the fact that" to "that"* or *don't use fragments*—that many writing books are a bit too quick to proclaim. The passive can be deployed quite effectively. The previous sentence is an example, I would submit—certainly of the passive voice, but also of not-at-all-bad writing. Not only is it perfectly okay as is, but if you switched to active, you would produce a dull monstrosity along the lines of: *Many writers deploy the passive voice quite effectively.* Who are these faceless writers? (Take a memo: we're adding *many* to the list of words that should be avoided if possible.)

Putting the matter in general terms, the passive is fine if your emphasis is properly on the object of the verb, rather than the subject, or if a quality of the subject isn't knowable. The passive *President Kennedy was shot earlier today* is better than the active *An unknown gunman shot President Kennedy earlier today.*

The passive is a problem if and only if it leaves in its wake an insistent question that begins with the word *Who?* The classic non-apology-apology was made famous, if not originated, by Ron Ziegler, President Nixon's press secretary, in 1973, in reference to what he had previously said about the *Washington Post*'s Watergate coverage: "We would all have to say that mistakes were made in terms of comments." That quote went down in history because Ziegler tried to fudge the key point: who made the mistakes?

Scientific writing apparently demands the passive voice. However, in other forms, it should be used sparingly. In the passage below, it appears four times in three sentences.

> [*Because the peppercorns were contaminated (1) with the bacteria, a recall was issued (2) on all of the contaminated salami. 1.3 million pounds were recalled (3). The product was destroyed (4) under supervision by specialists.*]*

In my judgment, 1 is fine, 2 is bad, and the last two are borderline. But the passage can only sustain one passive, so I would get rid of 3 because it's easily changed. So a possible rewrite could be.

> *The Centers for Disease Control issued a recall on all contaminated salami, and eventually, 1.3 million pounds were recalled. CDC specialists destroyed the meat.*

---

* In addition, "contaminated salami" is a kind of passive adjective, being shorthand for "salami that has been contaminated."

9. WHAT THE MEANING OF "IS IS" IS

Redundant is almost always hurled as a negative epithet indicating repetitiveness or tautology, but it can be an effective rhetorical device. Shorn of all redundancy, Shakespeare's "most unkindest cut of all" would be pretty vanilla and the ad slogan "Raid Kills Bugs Dead" would become the ho-hum "Raid Kills Bugs." Meanwhile, Gertrude Stein's "Rose is a rose is a rose is a rose" would have to be completely erased because the quotation is nothing *but* redundancy. (*Completely erased* is redundant as well—something is either erased or it isn't. But I felt like I needed the emphasis provided by *completely.*)

Most of the time, however, redundancy is mindless and bad, an instance of a writer reflexively putting down multiple words all denoting the same thing. It's tough to prove, but I have little doubt that redundancy is on the upswing, a manifestation of the wordiness and clunkiness that characterizes much writing these days. An example—in spoken English, certainly—is the phrase *is is*. A second *is* is usually (though not always—see the fourth word of this sentence) both redundant and superfluous. I just searched the phrase *is is* on National Public Radio's Web site and was presented with 1,810 hits. The most recent are:

> *And the media loves those hundred-million-dollar numbers. The reality is is that it's worth a lot less—35.5 million guaranteed.* (Sports correspondent Stefan Fatsis, on *All Things Considered.*)

> *But the truth is, is it's no longer insurance if the government says they're always going to bail you out.* (Representative Ron Paul, on *Talk of the Nation.*)

> *The big difference is, is that right now farmers—and other employees, actually, too—are not required to verify the information.* (*Milwaukee Journal Sentinel* reporter Georgia Pabst, on *Tell Me More.*)

And, to go to the other side of the political spectrum, here's a question from Fox News's Greta Van Susteren that's not only redundant, it's not a question:

> *The second question is, is that the* Wall Street Journal *is a very sort of elite big corporate-type newspaper, lots of money.*

Maybe that extra word seems like a hedge against misunderstanding, or maybe it just comes along with the prolixity of the age. In any case, it should go.

I have started to note, in my students' work and in all sorts of published work, the blooming of a lot of other phrases that are equally redundant, though not as obviously so.

> [*My mouth continued to remain open.*]

> *My mouth remained open.*

[We're celebrating our two-year anniversary next week.]

We're celebrating our second anniversary next week. (*Anniversary* has the same root as *annual* and implies a commemoration of a certain number of *years*. That said, it's okay to use phrases like *two-month anniversary,* if you really must.)

———————

[I really appreciate the effort put in by my fellow classmates.]

I really appreciate the effort put in by my classmates. (*Fellow countrymen, fellow colleagues,* and *fellow teammates* are similar redundancies that need to lose the *fellow.*)

———————

[The rules apply to both men and women alike.]

The rules apply to men and women alike.

———————

[The play is well written, but yet it contains far too many clichés.]

The play is well written, but it contains too many clichés.

Even still to start a sentence (*Even still, the wedding was a success*) is kind of a redundancy in that it welds together two synonymous expressions—*even so* and *still*. They are both fine; pick one.

10. TONE

Imagine that you're invited to a pool party and you wear a formal gown. Or you're invited to a fancy wedding and you wear madras shorts and a Philadelphia Eagles jersey. In each case your ensemble may be perfectly matched and generally speaking spot-on, but all wrong for the occasion.

The same goes for writing. Each form or genre you will work in has its own stylistic dress code, another word for which is *register*. Some of the variables are word choice, length of sentence, length of paragraph, and relative comfort with contractions and with a conversational tone, or even slang. There are subtle variations even between similar genres. Newspaper reporters favor short words and paragraphs, but a fairly formal tone: they ~~wouldn't~~ would not ~~employ~~ use contractions. Magazine writers, on the other hand, are fond of long sentences and paragraphs, and a conversational tone that can veer off into the breezy and slick. And in an academic paper or book, it is expected that the writer will potentially proceed in violation of virtually all the precepts outlined in this volume! But no exclamation points allowed.

To avoid being that person in the loud shorts, it's necessary to case the joint in advance. That is to say, read the best practitioners in the genre you want to contribute to. Maybe even copy down some of their sentences and paragraphs. Eventually you'll get a feel for the expectations, and start to dress the part.

D. Sentence to Sentence, Paragraph to Paragraph

So can I assume we're all good on sentences? Mazel tov! As we move on to subsequent sentences, and then paragraphs, the key issues are cadence or rhythm, variety, novelty, consistency, and transitions.

The first two (and a lot else besides) are taken up in the beginning of one of my all-time favorite quotes about writing, from the pen of the critic F. W. Bateson. I like the rest of the quote, too, so here's the whole thing:

> [The] defining characteristics of good prose [are]: a preference for short sentences diversified by an occasionally very long one; a tone that is relaxed and almost colloquial; a large vocabulary that enjoys exploiting the different etymological and social levels of words; and an insistence on verbal and logical precision.

Relatively short sentences should be the default, as Bateson suggests, but too many of them in a row produces a staccato ersatz-Hemingway sound, or a dumbed-down Dick-and-Jane sort of thing. Not only will you be able to hear this when you read them aloud, but you can learn to literally see the problem—the short sentences will jump out at you. To fix this, just link the sentences together with commas, conjunctions (*and, but*), and/or logical connectors like *although, after,* or *because*.

> [*The store will open its doors tomorrow. Baseball star Albert Pujols will give a speech. The first ten customers will receive signed baseballs.*]

At the store's opening ceremony tomorrow, baseball star Albert Pujols will give a speech. The first ten customers will receive autographed baseballs.

A series of long sentences is even worse. Not only does rhythm go by the boards, but it quickly becomes hard for the reader to make his or her way. It's like walking in the jungle and finding that all of a sudden the vegetation has gotten impassably thick. Fortunately, chopping up sentences is usually pretty easy. I certainly spend a lot of my revising time doing just that. Take a look at the first draft of a passage in this book:

[If you're on one side or the other and trying to stoke the fire on any of these issues, go nuts with the terms I've been discussing and the many others like them. However, if you're writing in an intelligent, nonpartisan way, avoid them at all costs, instead seeking words that accurately and temperately convey meaning, such as legalized abortion, government spending, taxes (in general) and the estate tax (in particular).]

Reading it aloud, I could see something was off with the second sentence. Like a rapper or basketball player, I tend to try for a strong "flow," hence the phrase *instead seeking* and what came after (a lot). But I could tell that right about there, I had to shut the faucet off.

If you're on one side or the other and trying to stoke the fire on any of these issues, go nuts with the terms I've been discussing and the many others like them. However, if you're writing in an intelligent, nonpartisan way, avoid them at all costs. Instead, seek out words that accurately and temperately convey meaning, such as legalized abortion, government spending, taxes (in general), and the estate tax (in particular).

Follow a similar strategy with paragraphs. If you scan down the screen or the page, and they all seem to be roughly the same size, work on varying them. It's usually easy to fuse two short paragraphs together. Breaking a long one up can be more challenging, but you can generally discern a sort of point of perforation where it can be divided. If you can't, leave it be.

By *novelty*, I mean don't repeat words, phrase structures, figures of speech, or ideas. By the same token, you should make sure to maintain the tone or register of your writing; that's a matter of being consistent.

Sentence to sentence or paragraph to paragraph, transitions are a challenge. Certainly, standards differ according to what you are writing and your own style. A traditional essay requires a lot of transitional words and phrases along the lines of *consequently, needless to say, however,* and *furthermore.* However, transitions are famously not allowed in the traditional inverted-pyramid newspaper article. Whatever the form, the most important thing is to have a strong sense in your own mind of the relationship of one sentence or paragraph to the next. Sometime you'll have to specify the relationship, sometimes you won't. If you don't spell out enough, you'll drop one non sequitur after the other and generally baffle readers. But if you spell out too much, you may come off as ponderous, too literal, and almost overprotective, like a parent who leads his child by the hand even though the kid is a high schooler. Ultimately, as with so much else, it's a mama bear, papa bear, and baby bear kind of thing: you're the one who has to decide what's just right. If you turn off the music, you're mindful, and you read, read, read, you can do it.

AUTHOR'S NOTE

This is my third book about words. They've come in kind of a weird order. The first, *The Sound on the Page: Style and Voice in Writing*, dealt with some rather advanced matters and took as object lessons the very best writers, now and through history. The second, *When You Catch an Adjective, Kill It: The Parts of Speech, for Better and/or Worse*, was about, among other things, the cool and expressive things all sorts of people do with the English language, things like using the word *chill* as a noun, adjective, and verb (transitive and intransitive). And now I'm telling you how to not write bad. I shudder to think what the next book will be.

In a way, I've been working on this book for twenty years, which is how long I've been teaching writing at the University of Delaware. The job has been a picture window on the way people write now—and by *people* I mean bright students at a selective university who have elected to take advanced journalism and other writing classes. There are some nice views out that window, but on the whole the picture isn't pretty. As the years and the articles, essays, assignments, papers, and other assignments built up, I came to realize that my students, generally speaking, were not adept. Writing well was not the task at hand for most of them. A more pressing need was getting rid of their bad habits and getting acquainted with some core principles.

Helping them achieve this has been a challenge that, as Dr. Johnson would put it, concentrated my mind wonderfully. It made me think about writing in new ways, and appreciate it in new ways, too. I believe the other teachers out there will back me up when I say that nothing in my professional life is more gratifying than reading a great piece of work by a student—unless it's reading a great piece of work by a student who started out the semester not that great. I still remember an article written in my very first class in 1992. It was Tye Comer's on-the-scene piece about a "rave"—then a phenomenon so new that it demanded quotation marks. It was fantastic, and I gave it a well-deserved A+. I remember so many other outstanding pieces over the years, including lines that knocked me out when I read them and get me misty-eyed when I think back on them. So thanks to those who gave me such pleasure, and to all of you, for what you helped me to figure out.

A secondary pleasure has been following the careers of some of these folks. (Tye, for example, is an editor and writer with *Billboard* magazine; I've just been enjoying reading his posts from the Coachella Festival, which, come to think of it, is a rave of sorts.) Some I've become friends with, including Jocelyn Terranova, who provided excellent research assistance for this book, as she has for others of mine. Another student from those early years is Devin

Harner, now a fellow journalism professor and a welcoming sounding board for ideas and problems.

I think of my colleagues from the University of Delaware as teammates, always ready to throw me a buddy pass or call my number in the huddle. I have had many fun and fruitful conversations about writing with Debby Andrews, Dee Baer, Steve Bernhardt, Jim Dean, Dawn Fallik, McKay Jenkins, Kevin Kerrane, Don Mell, Charley Robinson, and lots of others in Memorial Hall. John Jebb, going above and beyond the call of duty, deaccessioned a few volumes from his vast library on writing, and gave them to me. Linda Stein and Susan Brynteson, of UD's proper library, were greatly supportive. Beyond campus, I've benefited from conversations and e-mail exchanges with Bruce Beans, Wes Davis, David Friedman, John Grossmann, John Marchese, Geoffrey Pullum, and Bill Stempel.

I'd like to thank some editors who gave me the opportunity to work out some of these ideas in pieces for their publications: Heidi Landecker, Liz McMillen, and Jean Tamarin at the *Chronicle of Higher Education*; Juliet Lapidos and Julia Turner at *Slate*; and Whitney Dangerfield at the *New York Times*.

Thanks to Geoff Kloske and Laura Perciasepe at Riverhead Books for helping this book find its best self; and to Stuart Krichevsky, Shana Cohen, and their colleagues at the Stuart Krichevsky Literary Agency for, well, you know.

Last and best, thanks always to Gigi Simeone, Elizabeth Yagoda, and Maria Yagoda, my posse.